MISSION
SHARK RESCUE

A school of fish swirls around a whale shark near Yucatán, Mexico.

MISSION SHARK RESCUE

ALL ABOUT SHARKS AND HOW TO SAVE THEM

RUTH A. MUSGRAVE WITH NATIONAL GEOGRAPHIC EXPLORER DANIEL RAVEN-ELLISON

NATIONAL GEOGRAPHIC KIDS

WASHINGTON, D.C.

Caribbean reef sharks live in reefs in the Bahamas and South America.

>> CONTENTS

NATIONAL GEOGRAPHIC KiDS

MISSION ANIMAL RESCUE

Save ANIMALS >> Save the WORLD

Lions and *Tigers* and *Polar Bears*—oh, my! Be sure to check out the other titles in the Mission Animal Rescue series. Available on bookshelves near you.

MISSION ANIMAL RESCUE

At National Geographic we know how much you care about animals. They enrich our planet—and our lives. Habitat loss, hunting, and other human activities are threatening many animals across the globe. The loss of these animals is a loss to humanity. They have a right to our shared planet and deserve to be protected.

With your help, we can save animals—through education, through habitat protection, and through a network of helping hands. I firmly believe the animals of the world will be safer with us on their side.

Throughout this book and the other books in the Mission Animal Rescue series, you'll see animal rescue activities just for kids. If you go online at natgeo.com/kids/mission-animal-rescue, you can join a community of kids who want to help animals as much as you do. Look for animal rescue videos, chats with explorers, and more. Plus, don't miss the dramatic stories of animal rescues in *National Geographic Kids* magazine.

We share our Earth with animals. Helping them means helping our planet and protecting our future.

Together we can do it.

—Daniel Raven-Ellison, *Guerrilla Geographer and National Geographic Explorer*

YOUR PURCHASE SUPPORTS ANIMALS AND THEIR HABITATS

The National Geographic Society is a nonprofit organization whose net proceeds support vital exploration, conservation, research, and education programs. Proceeds from this book will go toward the Society's efforts to support animals and their habitats. From building bomas for big cats to protect their wild territory to studying elephants and how they communicate to exploring wild places to better understand animal habitats, National Geographic's programs help save animals and our world. Thank you for your passion and dedication to this cause. To make an additional contribution in support of Mission Animal Rescue, ask your parents to consider texting ANIMAL to 50555 to give ten dollars. See page 112 for more information.

To catch its food, a nurse shark quickly sucks in its prey near Key Largo, Florida, U.S.A.

HELP SAVE SHARKS

Fast, fierce, and fascinating, sharks are top predators in the ocean. These sophisticated fish have existed for more than 350 million years. With their sleek design, razor-sharp teeth, and powerful jaws, they leave a big impression in their wake. These awe-inspiring creatures have a complicated relationship with humans.

They are often portrayed in movies and books as bloodthirsty killers on the hunt for people—and today's headlines continue to fuel that perception. But shark attacks on people are rare. Most of the more than 500 species of sharks stay away from people. Humans killing sharks, however, is another story. Many species of shark populations are declining. People kill as many as 100 million sharks each year. Some fragile shark populations have plummeted more than 90 percent and many are threatened with extinction.

Today, sharks are considered vulnerable and threatened in many parts of the world. Although sharks have been silently drifting toward extinction with little uproar, the tide is turning. People are starting to appreciate how important these predators are for the marine ecosystem—and for all of us. All over the world, governments, scientists, and concerned people like you are joining forces to protect these incredible fish.

Together we can create a plan to help save sharks. Rescue activities at the end of each chapter will help you learn how you can have a hand in conservation efforts. Sharks need you to become their advocate and voice so they can survive. Are you ready to dive in? Let's save sharks!

>> THROUGH A SHARK'S EYES

The summer sun sparkles on the electric blue water near Cat Island in the Bahamas. Just below the surface, butterflyfish, angelfish, and other brightly colored reef fish dart through the sea. Suddenly, out of the shadows, a dusky shark named Atlas appears. Unlike the quick smaller fish, he moves sluggishly. He's dying.

ALL TANGLED UP

Somewhere on his travels, the nearly seven-foot (2-m)-long shark became entangled in a discarded piece of net. It encircled his head like a rope necklace. Since sharks have fins, not hands, Atlas cannot remove the net. At first, the healthy young shark continued to hunt and swim. Eventually, though, the broken net caused problems for him.

Since the dusky shark population dropped in this area of the western Atlantic Ocean because of overfishing, it is now illegal for humans to hunt them here. Scientists hope the population rebounds in this important nursery area for baby dusky sharks. However, dusky sharks continue to die in nets and on longlines (set for prey that sharks also hunt). It's unknown how many sharks are trapped in discarded nets each year.

The rope wraps around Atlas's pectoral fins, the fins where our arms would be, pinning them against his body. Like all sharks, Atlas uses his pectoral fins for steering, stopping, agility, and balance. Without full use of his fins, he cannot maneuver well. Now the net is not just inconvenient, it's putting his life in jeopardy.

Divers remove the rope cutting into the neck of Atlas, a dusky shark.

A DUSKY SHARK MIGHT LIVE UP TO 45 YEARS.

With the rope removed, Atlas can begin to heal.

FROM PREDATOR TO PREY

Atlas continues to grow weaker and hunting becomes tougher. With every swish of his tail, the net cuts farther into his skin, slowly sawing him in half. The gash the rope has cut cannot heal as long as it remains in place. The rope also squeezes his gills, making it more difficult to get water over his gills and out the gill slits. Catching prey becomes harder and harder.

Like most sharks, Atlas is the very definition of self-sufficient. He hunts alone. He swims alone. There's no pack or herd to help him or to provide food. Normally, Atlas would eat a variety of fish, including tuna, mackerel, and eel. He also hunts octopuses, squid, smaller sharks, and rays. In his weakened state, however, catching any of these quick creatures is a monumental chore.

Life in the sea means that one moment an animal is the predator, and the next, prey. Large healthy sharks don't have many predators. The net and weakness hobble Atlas. No longer is Atlas powerful, stealthy, or agile enough to escape from a larger or even equal-size predator, like an oceanic whitetip or bull shark.

Skinny, weak, and swimming through shark-infested waters with an open wound means Atlas is in trouble.

THE SWEET SMELL OF FISH

As he meanders through the reef, a sound attracts Atlas's attention. Then he smells something delicious. Blood. By the amount bathing his nostrils, it's either a dead or injured fish. In his weakened state, it's the perfect dinner. The closer he gets, the stronger the water churns with blood.

Atlas approaches cautiously. Oceanic whitetips lurk in the area and the smell might also attract them. If he can get to the fish and then escape, he won't become a meal, too. The smell attracts him not to a floundering or decomposing fish but to a boat with people in and around it. The divers "chummed" the water, dropping bits of chopped fish and fish blood into the water to attract sharks. The people aren't there to hurt or hunt sharks. They just want a chance to view them up close. Tourists from all over the world visit the Bahamas every year to admire the beauty and grace of oceanic whitetip, silky, and dusky sharks. They even swim with them!

Atlas skirts around the boat and the divers in the water, still lured by the overpowering smell of food. Circling a few times, he swims away. Atlas must calculate his own risk before getting too close. He's weak and ungainly, and it would be an effort to fight or escape if he becomes a target.

Too risky, he decides. The hungry shark swims away.

The next day, once again enticed by the smell, Atlas finds the boat and humans. Maybe it is the way the humans behave, sound, or smell, but something causes him to let down his guard and come closer. Maybe hunger simply overpowers him. Atlas swims in between the divers and grabs some floating bits of fish. Then he rushes away. He circles back, returning to gobble more fish and then retreating into the shadows. He repeats this behavior a few more times.

After a while, when Atlas slows down for another bite, one of the divers carefully grabs the rope. Before Atlas can get away, something incredible happens. Another diver cuts the net. Atlas instantly feels relief, but the rope is still embedded in the deep wound. Atlas uses his limited strength to roll away and unravel the rope. Freedom, at last!

AN UNCERTAIN FUTURE

Although the humans have released Atlas from a slow death, he's thrust into a possibly quicker one. Just as he rolls away, finally unbound, five oceanic whitetips change course, rushing toward him. To them, he is an injured shark in water bloodied by chum. Such a dinner bell would pique any large shark's curiosity.

The divers shoo the curious sharks away.

Fortunately for Atlas, the sharks calmly swim off and go about their business. The rescuers save Atlas twice.

After eating and swimming near the divers for a few hours, Atlas disappears into the darkness. He is free of the rope, but now the deep open wound encircling his head fills the water with the scent of a weak, injured animal. Can he survive? The divers would have to wait and hope. Atlas has already proved he's tough and determined to survive.

> THE DUSKY SHARK'S SCIENTIFIC NAME, *CARCHARHINUS*, IS DERIVED FROM TWO GREEK WORDS MEANING "SHARP NOSE."

"SHARKS ARE AMONG THE MOST PERFECTLY CONSTRUCTED CREATURES IN NATURE."

—"SHARK LADY" EUGENIE CLARK, MARINE BIOLOGIST

CHAPTER 1

>> POWERFUL PREDATORS

A sand tiger shark can remain motionless in the water.

With an impeccably designed body formed by time and a watery home, nothing is more elegant than a shark. These flawless hunters have existed for more than 350 million years. From nose to tail, inside and out, sharks' finely tuned bodies have survived every change that has shaken the Earth and have allowed them to adapt to every habitat.

BUILT FOR THE SEA

There's nothing ordinary about a shark. This sleek and powerful predator is often the top predator in its habitat. There are more than 500 species of sharks. Sharks live in every ocean habitat on Earth, from ankle-deep water to the farthest depths. Some even live in freshwater rivers.

Sharks are fish. Like other fish, they have fins, gills, scales, and are cold-blooded, which means their body temperature matches the water's temperature. Several species keep their body temperature warmer than the temperature of their surroundings in order to keep their muscles and body warm and ready to hunt on a moment's notice. Nothing about a shark, though, is exactly like an ordinary fish. Take the skeleton, for example. Other fish, like goldfish, have skeletons made of bone. Sharks do not. Their skeleton, which has a backbone like other animals, is made of cartilage, the same tissue that shapes your ears. This flexible, light-weight, and strong material gives sharks an advantage over other fish dragging their heavy bony bodies through the sea.

Sharks' closest relatives include skates, rays, and the lesser known chimaera, or "ghost shark." They all belong to the scientific class called Chondrichthyes.

Sharks may seem like all angles and sharp edges, but everything about their body makes them as fluid as the water itself. A shark's sleek body means speed, agility, and power. Some sharks, like shortfin makos, rocket and weave through the water to outrace and

A shortfin mako shark's stream-lined body cuts through the water off the coast of California.

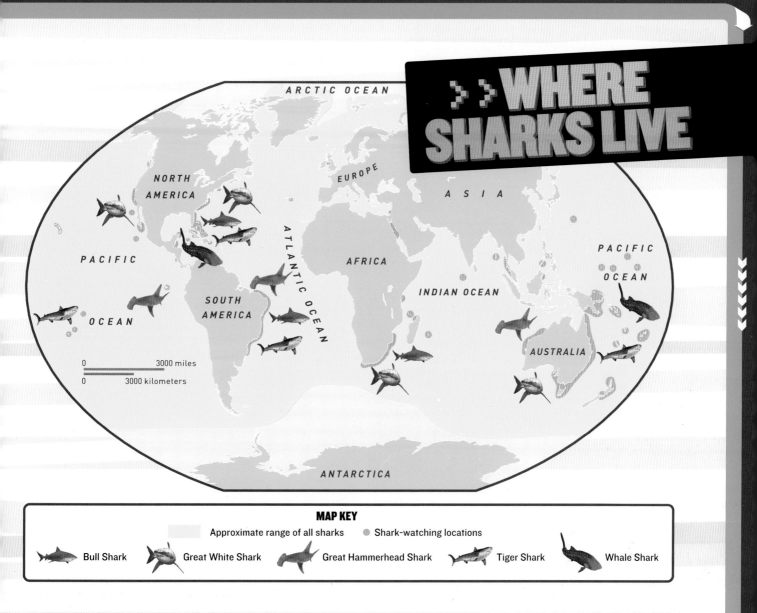

ARCTIC OCEAN

NORTH AMERICA

EUROPE

ASIA

PACIFIC OCEAN

ATLANTIC OCEAN

AFRICA

INDIAN OCEAN

PACIFIC OCEAN

SOUTH AMERICA

OCEAN

AUSTRALIA

0 ——— 3000 miles
0 ——— 3000 kilometers

ANTARCTICA

MAP KEY

Approximate range of all sharks   ● Shark-watching locations

Bull Shark   Great White Shark   Great Hammerhead Shark   Tiger Shark   Whale Shark

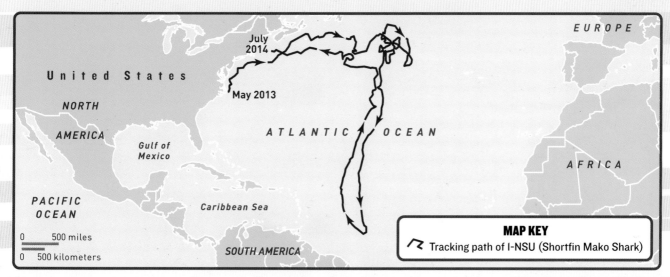

EUROPE

July 2014

United States

NORTH AMERICA

May 2013

ATLANTIC OCEAN

Gulf of Mexico

AFRICA

PACIFIC OCEAN

Caribbean Sea

0 ——— 500 miles
0 ——— 500 kilometers

SOUTH AMERICA

MAP KEY
↗ Tracking path of I-NSU (Shortfin Mako Shark)

Read about I-NSU on page 66.

SHARK VS. BONY FISH

Though they both have fins, scales, and gills, sharks and bony fish have adapted in different ways. Check out the differences.

A shark's skeleton is made of cartilage, the same tissue that forms your ears and nose.

Most fish skeletons are made of bone.

Sharks have five to seven gill slits. Sharks breathe (respire) by getting oxygen from the water when it passes over the gills and out the gill slits.

Bony fish, such as the lionfish, have fins that are bendy or fluttery and can fold against the body.

Bony fish have one gill opening. Scientists call this bony covering an operculum.

A shark does not have permanent scales or teeth. It loses and regrows its scales and teeth throughout its life.

As a bony fish grows larger, its scales grow larger, too.

Sharks' rigid fins do not bend. Pectoral fins help steer. The dorsal, pelvic, and anal fins provide stability and balance. The tail propels the shark through the water.

The brownbanded bamboo shark's coloration helps it hide on the sandy seafloor.

outmaneuver even the fastest prey. Other shark species, like angel sharks, may not swim fast, but they snatch prey with as much speed and precision. Angel sharks strike fast, snapping a fish from the water in about a tenth of a second—almost three times faster than the blink of an eye!

FINTASTIC FISH

Five kinds of fins enhance a shark's maneuverability and balance. As a spinner shark races through schools of fish, it uses all of its fins to spin like a drill. It uses its pectoral fins to steer, its tail fins to propel itself through the water, and the rest of the fins to help maintain its balance as it spins. While spiraling through the water, the shark gobbles fish without stopping. Spinner sharks move so fast, lucky beachgoers in Florida often see the impressive sharks vaulting into the air, still whirling at top speed.

Sharks move the tail fin side to side to swim. Fast sharks like makos, bull, and great whites have crescent-shaped tails with the top and bottom nearly equal in size. This tail shape gives the sharks extra power.

Not all sharks need to swim fast. Bamboo sharks

A spinner shark can make three full spins in the air before it crashes back into the sea.

use their large, strong, flexible pectoral and pelvic fins to creep across rocks and coral. Instead of a large tail for racing, the lower half of their tail is small, which makes it easier to hug the ocean floor.

Fins help sharks survive, but they can also cause their death. Throughout the world, people kill basking and many other shark species just for their fins.

FRICASSONCE

Every May, basking shark Fricassonce joins other sharks to court and feed in the plankton-rich water near the Isle of Man in the Irish Sea.

At 23 feet (7 m) long, Fricassonce is longer than a delivery truck, though basking sharks can reach lengths of up to 32 feet (10 m) and weigh 14,000 pounds (6,350 kg). While Fricassonce may not be the biggest basking shark, he's very important.

Fricassonce is helping scientists learn where basking sharks go after they leave the area in August. Basking sharks are critically endangered in some areas and threatened globally. Even before Fricassonce leaves the area, he gives the researchers a lot of information. When basking sharks mate, adult males rub up against the very rough skin of other sharks, leaving pink marks on their snouts. Fricassonce's size and freshly scrubbed pink snout show scientists he's a mature male of breeding age. In addition, the distinctive speckles on his dorsal fin—and the DNA that the scientists have collected—will help them identify him year after year. A satellite tag that biologists attached to his fin will track his movements for up to three years. The important information gathered helps scientists focus their conservation efforts.

When open, a basking shark's round mouth is larger than a hula hoop.

OCEAN CAMO

Sharks seem to appear and disappear like ghosts. Sharks' coloration conceals them in the dusky sea, keeping them camouflaged from predators and prey. Steel gray, blue, bronze, brown, or black, a shark's coloration varies depending on the species and where it lives. Sharks that live on the ocean floor are often dappled to hide among the shadows, rocks, and coral. Sharks on the move, swimming rather than hiding on the ocean floor, have dark backs and white undersides. Seen from above, the darker back disappears into the dark sea; from below, the light underside blends in with the bright surface. A young tiger shark's vertical stripes help it disappear in the rippling streaks of light from the surface.

SUPERSCALES

Some might argue that sharks are all teeth. In a way, this is true. Millions of tiny toothlike scales create a suit of armor that protects the skin and body.

Unlike the scales on bony fish, a shark's scales are not permanent. The shark grows more scales as it grows larger. New scales replace those that fall off throughout the shark's life.

If you've ever fallen into the water with your clothes on, you know how hard it is to move. The clothes create resistance, called drag. Unlike clothes, the shark's flexible scales reduce drag, helping the shark slice through the water like a hot knife through butter. The scales bristle to aid in how the water flows over the body, adding to the shark's speed and agility. By subtly rising or flattening, the scales help a shark angle turns, allowing one side of the body to slow while the other goes faster.

If you rub your hand across a shark's back from its tail toward its head, it feels scratchy, like sandpaper. Throughout history, people used shark skin as

(continued on page 24)

>> ANIMAL RESCUE!

A SHARK PICTURE'S WORTH

Fortunately for sharks, when National Geographic photographer Brian Skerry first saw the movie *Jaws* as a kid, he wasn't afraid. He was inspired. Since then, learning about sharks has been a lifelong passion for Skerry. As a photojournalist specializing in marine wildlife, he has spent more than 10,000 hours underwater and met many sharks!

Several years ago, Skerry realized that the right photograph could make a difference in how people view sharks. He started a mission: to demystify sharks by showing their individual personalities. Every image he makes shows how each shark is engaging, graceful, and unique. By using his photography and sharing his stories, Skerry hopes to shine a light on sharks' importance as predators and prey, and their role in the ecosystem.

Not all of Skerry's photos show beauty. Some show the harsh reality for sharks. Skerry has learned that shedding light on this amazing animal's plight can lead to positive change. When the president of Chile asked to use one of Skerry's heartbreaking photos of a dead thresher shark wrapped in a net, it ended up having a huge impact. That presentation led to a ban on shark finning in Chile.

Brian Skerry believes people, including kids like you, can help sharks in many ways.

Marine biologist David Ebert swims among some graceful gray reef sharks.

>> MEMORABLE MOMENT

Every day is a new adventure, a new discovery—and each day is always different. I was recently involved in a study of gulper sharks. We used to think there were three different kinds living in different locations. But we found there's only one species found in several places. This may not seem like big news, but the conservation consequences are very important to future efforts to protect this species.

>> EXPLORER INTERVIEW

DR. DAVID EBERT

BORN: SAN JOSE, CALIFORNIA, U.S.A.
JOB TITLE: PROGRAM DIRECTOR, PACIFIC SHARK RESEARCH CENTER
JOB LOCATION: MOSS LANDING, CALIFORNIA, U.S.A.
YEARS WORKING WITH SHARKS: MORE THAN 30

How are you helping to save sharks?

I gather information about sharks, their life history, ecology, and biology, and other information that will help governments, scientists, fisheries, and others manage and protect shark populations. Also, I hope that my research will better inform the public on the role of these fascinating fish.

Favorite part of your job?

Searching for little-known or "lost" sharks are the best memories I have studying these animals. Going to remote parts of the world looking for species no one has ever heard of and at times discovering species that are new to science is very exciting. I also get to share knowledge. Recently, I spent time working with people in island communities in the western Indian Ocean helping to improve the identification of the local sharks, rays, and chimaeras. It is great to pass along this knowledge, knowing it helps protect species by having local people watching for different sharks.

Where do you study sharks?

Much of my current efforts are focused in the western Indian Ocean and the waters around southern Africa, but who knows where else my search might take me one day. That is the fun part: I never know where I might be going next, but I am sure it will be somewhere exciting and interesting.

How can kids prepare to do your job one day?

Study hard, do well in school, and get as much experience as you can along the way. Get a well-balanced background, not just science, so you have all the skills you will need to work with sharks.

sandpaper, including Hawaiians, Maori, and early American cabinetmakers. Shark skin also was used on Japanese samurai sword handles to make them less slippery.

NO DENTIST, NO PROBLEM

The sight of a shark's open mouth with so many teeth showing might unnerve some people. Sharks have many rows of razor-sharp teeth (most have 20 to 30 rows), making their mouths as dangerous as a bowl of broken glass. But only if you're its prey or you unwisely reach inside! Fortunately, people are not on any shark's menu.

Some sharks swallow their food whole. Others use their teeth to seize, slice, gouge, crush, or saw food into smaller pieces.

Sharks do not have permanent teeth. A shark loses and regrows teeth its entire life. When a shark loses a tooth, the tooth from the row behind moves forward and fills the empty space. Then a new tooth grows in the last row. How long it takes to replace a tooth depends on the shark. It takes five months for a lesser spotted dogfish to replace a tooth and only eight to ten days for a lemon shark.

A shark loses and regrows as many as 30,000 teeth throughout its lifetime! Compare that to people. As our permanent teeth grow in, we lose only 20 baby teeth.

SHARK SCHOOL

Little is known about the family or social life of most sharks. Even the most recognizable and studied species, such as whale sharks and great white sharks, are swimming secrets.

Many sharks, such as tiger sharks, spend their days alone. Some solitary species may interact with other sharks only when they are old enough to breed. Others are more social. Nurse and swell sharks sleep piled on top of each other. Some sharks school, which means they gather in groups, to hunt or breed. Blue sharks travel in groups of similar sharks. The school might consist of blue sharks of the same sex, size, or age. Even pregnant females school with other pregnant blue shark females. "Larger sharks, like sevengill sharks, sometimes hunt alone. Other times they hunt in packs to subdue larger prey," said David Ebert.

ON AVERAGE, SCIENTISTS DISCOVER A NEW SHARK SPECIES EVERY TWO WEEKS.

Tawny nurse sharks pile up for a nap in a rocky hollow in the Andaman Sea off the coast of Myanmar.

SUPERSTAR SHARKS

Sharks come in all shapes and sizes.

A whale shark can reach a maximum length of 65 feet (20 m).

Shortfin makos' recorded speed is 30 miles an hour (48 km/h), but they may swim as fast as 46 miles an hour (74 km/h).

The ten-foot (3-m)-long pelagic thresher shark's tail is as long as its body. It stuns and kills prey by whipping its tail.

A basking shark's pectoral fins can be six feet (2 m) long.

>> EXPERT TIPS

Marine biologist David Ebert's tips on what it takes to save sharks:

1 Be ready for a challenging and exciting career that requires passion.

2 Be prepared for a lot of hard work.

3 You'll need a curious mind that comes up with bold ideas or new ways to make discoveries.

A Caribbean reef shark grabs a delicious lionfish for dinner.

Schools of leopard sharks may join forces with dog-fish and smoothhound sharks to hunt. Whether they're the same species or different, size seems to help determine dominance or hierarchy.

Scientist Johann Mourier (you'll read more about him on page 55) discovered that blacktip reef sharks form social groups of preferred "friends." Another research project found that lemon sharks also seem to have friends. An advantage to such companions might include learning from each other about where to find food, which predators to avoid, and other life lessons.

Friends? Hunting parties? Every day new discoveries give us a peek into sharks' remarkable social lives.

THE AGELESS SHARK

Another mystery for scientists is figuring out how long sharks live. Scientists use bones, teeth, and scales to figure out a fish's age. However, since sharks don't have bones, permanent teeth, or scales, those clues aren't available. There isn't a simple way to determine a shark's age. Currently, the most common method is to count growth rings from a cross section of their back-bone. However, sharks grow at different rates, so, unlike the annual growth rings of a tree, a single shark growth ring might represent one year or three years. Scientists need to understand life span, growth rates, and reproductive ages to help manage populations and improve conservation efforts.

KEYSTONE PREDATORS

Throughout the ages, sharks' important role as predators and prey has remained a constant. Sharks continue to play a crucial role in nearly every ocean ecosystem. Many ocean animals rely on sharks for food. Sharks are also important predators. Many are apex predators. That's an animal at the top of the food chain, with few if any predators. Healthy adult great whites, oceanic whitetip, and sixgill sharks are apex predators. Like all predators, sharks help maintain a habitat's natural balance by keeping prey populations healthy and strong.

Sharks survived ice ages, earthquakes, volcanoes, and more without a backward glance. Nothing could stop them. Until now. Over the last century, unrestrained shark fishing, competition for food, and the expansion of humans into every corner of the ocean has caused shark populations to plummet. Not just one species, but many species feel the pressure.

The good news is that biologists, conservation organizations, individuals, and some governments are leading the way to protect sharks. The more people who care, the faster we help protect sharks. Join us and help save the sharks—let's make a big splash!

ANIMAL SUPERPOWERS

LIFE IN A FISHBOWL

YOUR GOLDFISH AND A SHARK ARE A LOT ALIKE, BUT THERE ARE SOME THINGS A GOLDFISH CANNOT DO, SUCH AS . . .

. . . CATCH A SEAL.

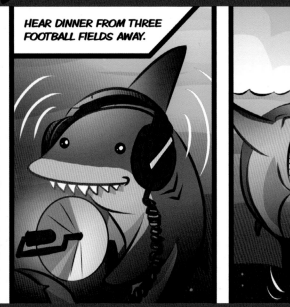

HEAR DINNER FROM THREE FOOTBALL FIELDS AWAY.

FRIGHTEN PEOPLE WITH JUST ONE FIN.

>>> RESCUE ACTIVITIES

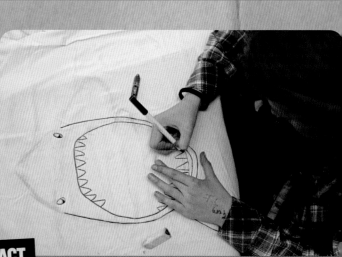

SAVE A PREDATOR

Sharks are among the top predators of the ocean, but they are also among the most hunted. People are killing sharks at extraordinary rates—sometimes on purpose and sometimes as accidental bycatch. Scientists, conservationists, and kids like you are teaming up to show the world what important animals sharks are for our oceans—and for the health of the entire planet. Create a campaign to save this vital group of fish.

ACT

START A PETITION

RESEARCH A CHANGE THAT COULD BE MADE THAT WOULD HELP TO SAVE SHARKS. National Geographic Explorer Enric Sala has helped create new sanctuaries, such as the world's largest single marine reserve in the South Pacific's Pitcairn Islands. Research how Sala achieved his success.

IDENTIFY A SENIOR DECISION-MAKER WHO CAN HELP TO MAKE THE CHANGE NEEDED. They could be a politician, business owner, or someone else. You could pick someone who you feel could or wants to do more, or someone who is already doing great work and you would like to thank.

WRITE A PETITION ASKING A DECISION-MAKER TO DO MORE TO SAVE SHARKS. Make sure you describe the problem, explain why it matters, and be specific about what you would like them to do.

MAKE

ORGANIZE A TEAM

BUILD A CAMPAIGN TEAM. You are far more likely to be successful if you have a good, strong, and reliable group. Campaigning on your own can be effective, too, but you will still need help from others to achieve your goal.

READ THIS BOOK FROM FRONT TO BACK, PLUS ARTICLES, VIDEOS, AND MORE. Become an expert on the problems that sharks face and how you can help them. Agree on the aim of your campaign.

DECIDE ON A CAMPAIGN NAME. You will also need a logo and slogan. You could draw these onto T-shirts, badges, or stickers.

Here are just three of the things that can be done by decision-makers to help save sharks:

SHARE

COLLECT SIGNATURES ON YOUR PETITION

BROWSE THE RESCUE ACTIVITIES AT THE END OF EACH CHAPTER IN THIS BOOK. You can use each activity as a way to raise attention for your campaign and collect signatures for your petition.

WITH A PARENT'S HELP, CONSIDER PUTTING YOUR PETITION ONLINE. There are many websites that allow you to create online petitions for free. Use this approach and you will have a global audience.

START BY ASKING YOUR FAMILY AND FRIENDS TO SIGN YOUR PETITION. Be prepared to answer any questions that they may have.

1 Do not eat, trade, sell, or process shark fins. Governments can make all of these illegal.

2 Use fishing techniques that reduce the chances of sharks being caught as bycatch.

3 Help in the creation of new marine conservation areas where people cannot catch sharks.

CHAPTER 2

>> WORLD OF SHARKS

Depending on where they live, great hammerhead sharks eat rays, sharks, lobsters, squid, crabs, and many kinds of bony fish.

"THE THING THAT CONSTANTLY JUMPS OUT IS HOW LITTLE WE STILL UNDERSTAND ABOUT SHARKS."

—MAHMOOD SHIVJI, SHARK BIOLOGIST

Point to any ocean location on a globe, and you'll find a shark population. Whether it's a coral reef, kelp forest, polar sea, or your favorite ocean beach, sharks live there.

EPIC ANCIENT SHARKS

Since sharks first appeared hundreds of millions of years ago, the world has experienced ice ages, meteors, earthquakes, growing and shrinking seas, and more. While these earth-shattering and sometimes cataclysmic events happened, sharks quietly roamed the seas. These environmental changes led to the extinction of some shark species and allowed others to flourish.

Most of shark history has been lost in time—including the ancient "first shark," a direct link to today's sharks. That's because, unlike bones, the cartilaginous skeleton of sharks rarely fossilizes. Usually only sharks' teeth, and sometimes scales, will fossilize. This makes it hard for scientists to create pictures of what these ancient animals looked like.

Based on fossilized teeth, however, paleontologists know prehistoric sharks ranged in size, just like today's sharks. The most famous prehistoric shark, *Carcharocles megalodon,* nicknamed megalodon or megatooth, ruled the sea about 2 to 17 million years ago. That's hundreds of millions of years after sharks first appeared.

This colossal predator reached lengths up to 60 feet (18 m)—as long as a boxcar! Paleontologists estimate it devoured 2,500 pounds (1,134 kg) of food a day. That's like eating 3,300 cans of tuna every day. Though often compared to it in popular media, the great white shark cannot even begin to fill the megalodon's fins. It would take 30 large great whites to reach the weight of a single megalodon.

The megalodon is an example of a shark that couldn't adapt to the ever changing world. Unlike people, animals cannot move to a new location or shop at a different store when their surroundings change. Megalodons were adapted for warmer water, ate enormous marine mammals, and required a lot of food. Paleontologists think that when the climate changed a couple million years ago and the larger marine mammals moved into colder waters, the megalodons were left behind without enough food to survive.

MEGALODON
(now extinct)

GREAT WHITE SHARK

SKATES AND RAYS, SHARK COUSINS, FIRST APPEAR IN THE FOSSIL RECORD ABOUT 150 MILLION YEARS AGO.

As shown in this illustration, the prehistoric megalodon shark was three times longer than today's great white shark.

A fossilized tooth from the pre-historic megalodon shark. Like today's sharks, megalodons did not have permanent teeth.

RULERS OF THE SEA

Sharks thrive at every ocean depth, from the deepest point to water so shallow it barely covers our feet. Sharks even live in some rivers and a couple of lakes. They inhabit tropical, subtropical, temperate, and polar waters.

Though sharks may live everywhere, most people will never come near a shark unless they visit an aquarium. Hundreds, even thousands, of feet of water separate your toes from most sharks' homes. That's because most sharks, more than half of them, live more than 700 feet (213 m) deep. That distance would be like you standing on top of a 70-story-tall building with the sharks wandering the sidewalk below.

MEET THE SHARKS

Most people can count the number of shark species they know on one hand. The big five are great white, bull, tiger, hammerhead, and whale shark. Four notorious headline grabbers and a giant. Many would be surprised to discover there are more than 500 different kinds of sharks. Most species could comfortably fit in your bathtub—with room to spare!

Sharks range in size from gigantic to tiny. People travel around the globe to swim with the world's largest shark, the whale shark. The average length of this strikingly colored fish is about 32 feet (10 m). But some might reach lengths up to 65 feet (20 m)! That's the length of four sports utility vehicles. The beauty, size, and calm nature of this elegant creature captures worldwide interest,

>> FAMILY TREE

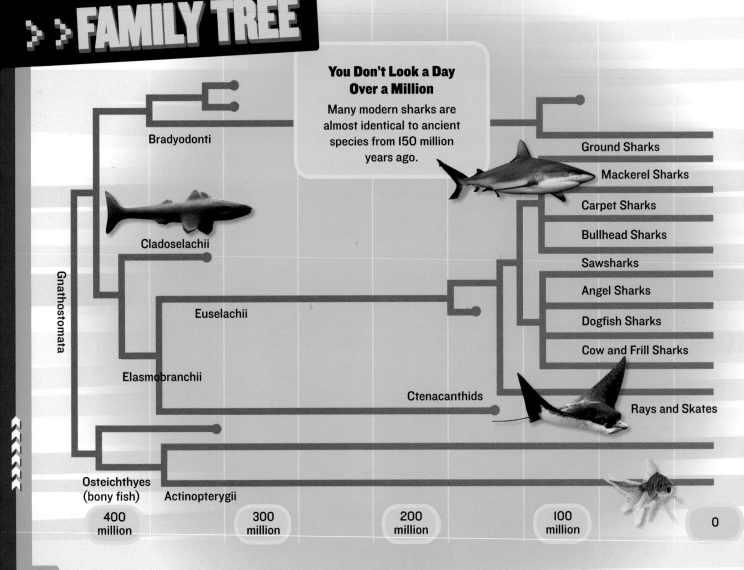

You Don't Look a Day Over a Million

Many modern sharks are almost identical to ancient species from 150 million years ago.

Bradyodonti

Cladoselachii

Euselachii

Elasmobranchii

Ctenacanthids

Gnathostomata

Osteichthyes (bony fish)   Actinopterygii

Ground Sharks

Mackerel Sharks

Carpet Sharks

Bullhead Sharks

Sawsharks

Angel Sharks

Dogfish Sharks

Cow and Frill Sharks

Rays and Skates

400 million	300 million	200 million	100 million	0

This illustration gives us an idea of what the prehistoric Hubbell's white shark might have looked like.

>> **MEET A SHARK**

HUBBELL'S WHITE SHARK

About 6.5 million years ago, a Hubbell's white shark hunted along the Peruvian coast. The warm tropical water was rich with fish, mollusks, crabs, whales, dolphins—even marine sloths. The 16-foot (5-m)-long shark ancestor ate fish and marine mammals.

It hunted closer to shore to avoid becoming prey. Two unstoppable superpredators also roved the ancient sea at that time, the megalodon shark (*Carcharocles megalodon*) and the giant sperm whale (*Livyatan melvillei*), with 1-foot (30-cm)-long teeth. Both predators were about 60 feet (18 m) long, more than three times as long as a Hubbell's.

The Hubbell's white shark found a perfect meal: a baleen whale carcass. It took a bite from the meaty part of the head, breaking a tooth off in the whale's jawbone. Like modern sharks, this ancient shark had rows of sharp teeth, none of them permanent. The shark then devoured the blubber, swallowing whole chunks of fat. This feast provided it with so much energy, the fortunate shark did not need to eat again for several days.

What happened next is still unknown. But millions of years later, in Peru, where the Hubbell's fossil was discovered, paleontologists also found a whale's skeleton with a Hubbell's shark tooth still imbedded in the jaw, giving them an important glimpse into a moment long ago.

WEIRDEST SHARKS

Not all sharks are sleek beauties like a blue shark. Some dare to be different. Meet some wild and weird sharks.

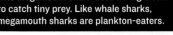
The megamouth shark uses its big mouth to catch tiny prey. Like whale sharks, megamouth sharks are plankton-eaters.

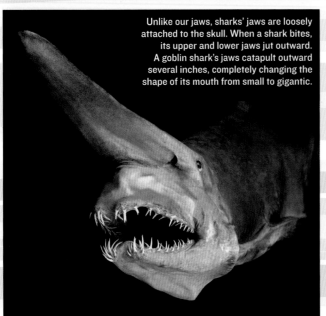

Unlike our jaws, sharks' jaws are loosely attached to the skull. When a shark bites, its upper and lower jaws jut outward. A goblin shark's jaws catapult outward several inches, completely changing the shape of its mouth from small to gigantic.

The rare frill shark looks less like a shark and more like an eel with its extra-long frilly gill slits.

The longnose sawshark swims through a school of fish, slashing and stunning prey with its tooth-covered snout.

With its odd-looking head, the scalloped hammerhead has better depth and distance perception that gives it a 360-degree view of the ocean.

making it one of the few popular and beloved sharks.

A few sharks, including great whites and great hammerheads, reach lengths around 18 feet (5 m), the length of about three adult humans.

But a three-year-old child is longer than most kinds of sharks. Some could even fit in your hand! Like the 6.6-inch (16.8-cm)-long dwarf lantern shark, one of the smallest sharks in the world. A newborn lantern shark is the length of your index finger. Like most sharks, dwarf lantern sharks live in the deep sea.

OCEAN OLYMPIANS

The ocean covers 70 percent of the Earth, but it's much more than what we see at the surface. Just as there are habitats on land, the ocean has many habitats, including coral reefs, seaweed forests, sea grass meadows, open ocean, and deep sea.

Throughout time, sharks expanded into these different habitats to take advantage of new food sources, less competition for food, or habitats with fewer predators.

Sharks moved into the reefs, like Australia's Great Barrier Reef. Here, the retreating tide traps animals in shallow pools of water. A hungry epaulette shark searches for food in one pool. The slender shark, about the size of a loaf of French bread, wriggles underneath rocks and between coral searching for worms and crabs. Unable to find food in that tide pool, it scrambles out of the water. Using its large pectoral and pelvic fins, it waddles across the rocks and slips into another pool.

Other sharks revel in warm sunny seas thousands of miles from the nearest shore. The stocky oceanic whitetip shark swims near the surface with its friends, such as pilot whales.

(continued on page 40)

During the Census of Marine Life, scientists studied a variety of ocean animals and habitats.

>> ANIMAL RESCUE!

COUNTING OCEAN ANIMALS

Between 2000 and 2010, 2,700 scientists from 80 countries participated in a monumental marine scientific endeavor called the Census of Marine Life. This first-of-its-kind project studied and identified animals in every part of the sea and compiled the most comprehensive inventory of ocean life in history, recording animals like octopus (top left), jellyfish (middle), and a northern elephant seal (bottom right).

In order to study migration, behavior, feeding, breeding, and more, scientists went on more than 540 expeditions and spent 9,000 days at sea. Through this global initiative, scientists rediscovered species thought to be extinct and discovered many no one knew existed. Prior to the census, scientists estimated 230,000 species lived in the ocean. Today, that estimate is closer to 250,000. (If microbes are included, there could be more than a million ocean species!)

What does this have to do with sharks? As humans forge ahead fishing—often overfishing, causing habitat destruction and touching every habitat—all ocean animals are vulnerable because of our lack of knowledge. The census provides information that lawmakers and scientists can use to protect the sea—and sharks!

Check out the census at coml.org.

>> EXPLORER INTERVIEW

DR. MICHELLE HEUPEL

BORN: ABERDEEN, SOUTH DAKOTA, U.S.A.
JOB TITLE: SENIOR RESEARCH SCIENTIST, AUSTRALIAN INSTITUTE OF MARINE SCIENCE
JOB LOCATION: AUSTRALIA
YEARS WORKING WITH SHARKS: 20

How are you helping to save sharks?

My research provides science that conservation managers and other people need to protect sharks. In the field, I also sometimes have to rescue sharks. Over the years, I've caught many sharks that had hooks, lines, pieces of net, or other items caught on their fins or in their mouth. If some of these items had stayed in place, the sharks would have died. I also have captured sharks with bites from other sharks. Because I do surgery for part of my work, I sewed the bite wounds shut to help them heal.

Best thing about working in the field?

The ability to see animals in their natural environment and gain an understanding of where they are and what they are doing. Being in the field on a beautiful day in clear water catching sharks is one of the best experiences.

How can kids prepare to do your job one day?

Take science, marine biology, and math courses in school and at university. These are the most important bases for becoming a marine biologist. Of course, some projects require learning to scuba dive!

Shark expert Michelle Heupel holds a gray reef shark during a research trip, just before she returns it back to the sea.

My favorite memory is of the first shark I tracked in Terra Ceia Bay, Florida, U.S.A. The project was a brand-new concept and we weren't sure it would work. The shark was a blacktip and a newborn— very small and extremely cute. I feel like that little shark and I started an adventure together. He stayed and swam around my study site for six months, helping me learn things we never knew about blacktip sharks. He even came back the next year—what a champion!

SHARKS DO NOT DIE IF THEY STOP SWIMMING.

RIP
SHARKWORTH
IF ONLY HE KEPT SWIMMING!

SHARKS DO NOT DEVOUR EVERYTHING THEY SEE.

EACH SPECIES HUNTS SPECIFIC FOODS AND IGNORES THE REST.

SHARKS DO NOT HUNT PEOPLE. WE ARE NOT ON ANY SHARK'S MENU.

>> EXPERT TIPS

Marine biologist Michelle Heupel's tips for how kids can help save sharks:

1 Get a good education and learn math, especially statistics!

2 Think about what questions you are interested in. This will help determine who you work with and where.

3 Be ready to go fishing. This often means getting wet, dirty, smelly, muddy, or all of the above!

Well, maybe not friends, but companions. Oceanic whitetips and the whales often swim and hunt together. Whitetips might take advantage of the pilot whales' excellent squid-locating skills.

Some sharks adapted to the cold. In the polar sea in the northern Atlantic, a huge Greenland shark lurks beneath the ice. The shark is about the length of a soccer goal, 24 feet (7.3 m). It eats everything from seals to cod, herring, salmon, and even sometimes moose carcasses that fall into the water.

Many sharks prefer the darkest, deepest part of the ocean, including a tiny shark known as the pygmy shark. It lives 32,604 feet (9,938 m) down. (That's about six miles [10 km].)

RIVER SHARKS

The world's rarest and least well known group of sharks live exclusively in freshwater. The five species of river sharks live in freshwater rivers in Indonesia, Malaysia, India, Myanmar, and Australia. All species are endangered or critically endangered.

River sharks have limited habitat and distribution. Habitat destruction, human development, pollution, and commercial and recreational fishing threaten all river shark populations. Little is known about the river sharks, since few have ever been found.

How little is known? It was only in 2010 that scientists proved the Borneo river shark really existed.

SHARK MASCOT IN THE ISLE OF MAN

Imagine 20 basking sharks, each nearly twice the size of your boat, splashing, spinning, and leaping clear out of the water. One swish of a massive tail could be dangerous to a human observer. But that doesn't stop basking shark experts biologist Jackie Hall and engineer Graham Hall.

After settling on the Isle of Man in the Irish Sea, the Halls wondered about the basking sharks they saw. They realized that no one had studied them, and what was worse, no one was protecting this incredible species. In 2004, on a shoestring budget, the couple created the Manx Basking Shark Watch (MBSW). It began as a citizen science program that invited locals to photograph and monitor the basking sharks seasonally feeding along the Isle of Man's nearly 100-mile (160-km) stretch of coastline.

The Halls soon expanded the MBSW's efforts to include satellite tagging and gathering DNA samples, revealing important information about their migrations.

They continue to coordinate public campaigns that have helped protect basking sharks. Due to the Halls' initiative, the Isle of Man citizens now proudly consider basking sharks their mascot and have become active participants in their protection.

Graham Hall prepares to attach a tracking tag to the dorsal fin of a basking shark.

The only known example of an Irrawaddy river shark is a 100-year-old museum specimen. So few river sharks have been found that scientists do not know what they eat, if they have predators, whether they travel up and down the river, or if they ever enter the ocean.

River sharks generally have tiny eyes, broad snouts, and slender sharp teeth. Some river sharks might reach lengths up to 9 feet (3 m), but few adults have been found to confirm average sizes.

Maybe you can be the one to discover the answers to all these questions and help save the elusive but important river sharks.

ON THE MOVE

The territory, or home range, of sharks varies. Some sharks are homebodies, like the horn shark found along the coast of California, U.S.A. It lives its entire life in an area the size of a basketball court. But others travel the world.

Biologists are just discovering that many shark species have no restrictions when it comes to distance or depth. Wearing the latest satellite and acoustic tracking technology, sharks have shown they freely cross national borders, hemispheres, even the Equator on their migrations.

Blue, mako, and other sharks follow the food. Blue sharks travel thousands of miles annually across the ocean. One blue shark, equipped with a satellite tracker, migrated from New York, U.S.A., all the way to Brazil, a distance of 4,304 miles (6,927 km).

Others, like great white sharks, hunt in one place and then travel long distances, possibly to breed in a different location. After hunting seal pups along the shores of central California, or Isla de Guadalupe, Mexico, great whites swim to the middle of the Pacific Ocean, where they gather in a location scientists nicknamed the "shark café." Some of these sharks then swim all the way to Hawaii, U.S.A. The following year, the sharks return to California and Mexico to hunt seals again.

Scientists are not yet sure what the sharks are doing in the middle of the ocean. However, these exciting kinds of discoveries help nations work together to conserve

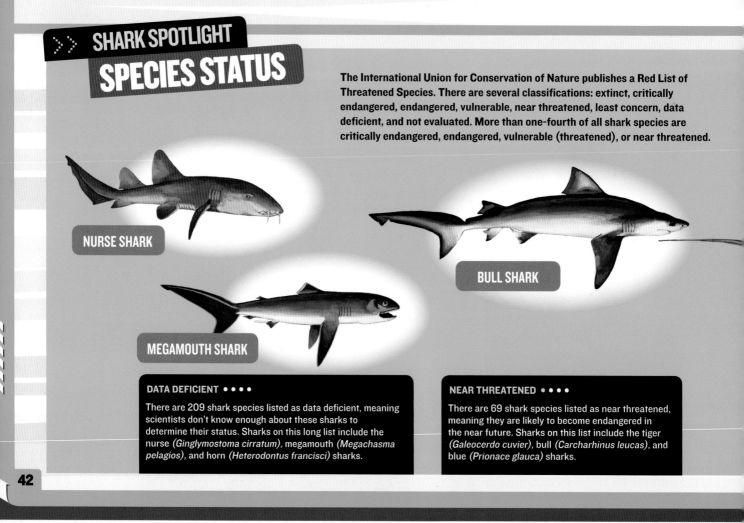

>> SHARK SPOTLIGHT
SPECIES STATUS

The International Union for Conservation of Nature publishes a Red List of Threatened Species. There are several classifications: extinct, critically endangered, endangered, vulnerable, near threatened, least concern, data deficient, and not evaluated. More than one-fourth of all shark species are critically endangered, endangered, vulnerable (threatened), or near threatened.

NURSE SHARK

BULL SHARK

MEGAMOUTH SHARK

DATA DEFICIENT ● ● ● ●
There are 209 shark species listed as data deficient, meaning scientists don't know enough about these sharks to determine their status. Sharks on this long list include the nurse (*Ginglymostoma cirratum*), megamouth (*Megachasma pelagios*), and horn (*Heterodontus francisci*) sharks.

NEAR THREATENED ● ● ● ●
There are 69 shark species listed as near threatened, meaning they are likely to become endangered in the near future. Sharks on this list include the tiger (*Galeocerdo cuvier*), bull (*Carcharhinus leucas*), and blue (*Prionace glauca*) sharks.

sharks by limiting the number of sharks taken from a population rather than from just one part of the world.

CONSERVING OUR OCEAN

The number one threat to sharks stems from fishing. As human populations grow, technology improves, and fishing techniques expand, we now interact with every ocean ecosystem across the seas and into the depths. Throughout the world, people compete with sharks for the same fish, squid, shrimp, and other seafood. When we overfish a food source, we make it harder for sharks to find enough food.

Commercial and recreational fishermen sometimes specifically target sharks for food or fins. Other times, sharks may just be in the wrong place at the wrong time. For example, people inadvertently kill Greenland sharks in nets and traps set for other fish. People call this accidental capture bycatch.

Though unintentional, bycatch has caused a significant drop in the Greenland shark population, causing the International Union for Conservation of Nature (IUCN) to classify it as near threatened.

Not so long ago, the oceanic whitetip was one of the most common top predators on Earth. Even though they live far from humans, oceanic whitetips are in trouble because of humans hunting them for their fins. Many whitetips also die in nets set for tuna and other fish. In just eight years, the oceanic whitetip population in the northwest and west-central Atlantic Ocean declined 70 percent. The IUCN regards oceanic whitetips as globally vulnerable, and critically endangered in the northwest and west-central Atlantic.

The threat to sharks is a worldwide crisis. Biologists consider at least one-fourth of all shark species threatened or endangered. Some shark populations have become locally extinct due to overfishing in one area.

Conservation changes have to come from people and their governments. Folks around the world are now searching for ways to find a balance between feeding people and protecting these important citizens of the sea so they can thrive for the future!

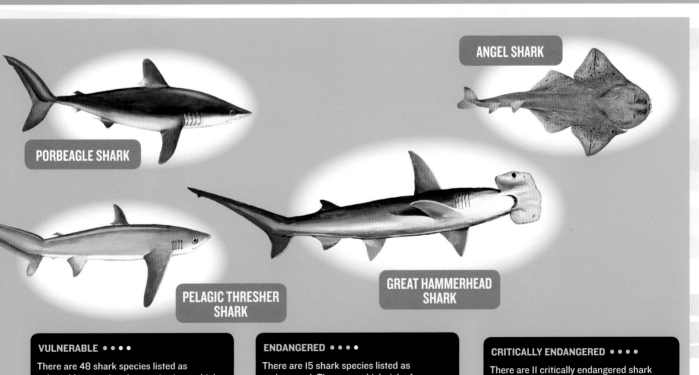

ANGEL SHARK

PORBEAGLE SHARK

PELAGIC THRESHER SHARK

GREAT HAMMERHEAD SHARK

VULNERABLE •••••
There are 48 shark species listed as vulnerable, meaning the species is at a high risk of becoming endangered. Sharks on this list include porbeagles (*Lamna nasus*), great whites (*Carcharodon carcharias*), and all three species of thresher (*Alopias*) sharks.

ENDANGERED •••••
There are 15 shark species listed as endangered. They are at high risk of becoming extinct. Sharks on this list include the great hammerhead (*Sphyrna mokarran*), Harrisson's gulper (*Centrophorus harrissoni*), and broadfin (*Lamiopsis temminckii*) sharks.

CRITICALLY ENDANGERED •••••
There are 11 critically endangered shark species. They are at the highest risk of extinction. Sharks on this list include the angel (*Squatina squatina*), daggernose (*Isogomphodon oxyrhynchus*), and three of the four species of river (*Glyphis*) sharks.

>>RESCUE ACTIVITIES

BE A STREET SHARK-IST

Sharks come in all shapes and sizes. Inspire people with a drawing, painting, sculpture, or another interpretation of a shark. Do this rescue activity by becoming a street artist and drawing attention to the story of sharks and how overfishing affects them as a species. You could use this activity as a way to collect names on your petition, too.

MAKE

MAKE DORSAL FINS

DRAW A SHARK'S DORSAL FIN ON PAPER OR CUT ONE OUT FROM CARDBOARD. This is the large famous fin that is on a shark's back and sometimes pokes out of the water. Pick a specific species, as different sharks have differently shaped dorsal fins.

DECIDE THE BEST WAY TO PHYSICALLY MAKE THE DORSAL FIN so that it can stand up on its own. You could make it from clay, papier-mâché, building blocks, or even dough.

MAKE THE DORSAL FIN. You could make the fin to scale, or keep its shape and make it much bigger or much smaller. Depending on how you have made your fin, you could make lots of them.

ACT

PUT ON A "SHARKTASTIC" SHOW

EXPLORE YOUR LOCAL AREA TO FIND A GREAT PLACE, such as a recreation center or school, to showcase your dorsal fin or fins. Pick a place where lots of people will see the fins.

HAVE FUN WITH POSITIONING YOUR FIN(S) in a way that makes it look like there is a shark swimming under the ground. You could shape sand, pebbles, or leaves to look like rippling water.

CONSIDER LEAVING A SMALL SIGN TO EXPLAIN WHY THE FIN IS THERE. Create a colorful and dramatic background to get people talking and have more of an impact.

44

Here are some tips for being a guerrilla artist:

1 Draw attention to your issue by putting something "out of place" in your art. A shark's fin on land will certainly get noticed!

2 Play with scale. More people will see models and drawings that are supersize.

3 Don't be afraid to set up your fin just to take a photo of it. More people may see the image that way rather than in person.

SHARE

SPREAD YOUR ART

TAKE PHOTOGRAPHS OF YOUR FIN. Then grab an adult and post the pictures online, like on National Geographic Kids' My Shot page (kids-myshot.nationalgeographic.com), along with a caption explaining what it means. If your petition is online, you can include a link to this, too.

BE EVEN MORE CREATIVE AND MAKE AN ANIMATION OF YOUR FIN. By taking lots of photos in order, you can make it look like your fin is swimming around.

SCALE UP YOUR ACHIEVEMENTS BY ASKING VISITORS TO MAKE THEIR OWN FINS. Every hour people kill about 11,000 sharks. Can you make even a fraction of this number?

This lemon shark pup hunts and hides in the tangled roots of the mangrove forest in Bimini, Bahamas.

CHAPTER 3

>> BORN TO SWIM

"REALIZING THAT SHARKS NEED PROTECTION IN EVERY OCEAN OF THE WORLD IS A FIRST IMPORTANT STEP IN CONSERVATION."

—JOHANN MOURIER, SHARK CONSERVATIONIST

Eyes open, teeth sharp, fins unfurled and only a minute old, the newborn lemon shark wastes no time swimming into the shadows and disappearing behind a gnarled tree root. The two-foot (61-cm)-long pup turns to watch its mother, a stocky yellowish gray shark, melt into the distance, leaving behind only a ripple. It may only be a few minutes old, but it knows two things: It must hunt to live, and something is probably already hunting it.

CONGRATULATIONS: IT'S A BABY SHARK

Some sharks hatch from eggs. Some sharks are born live. After giving birth or laying eggs, the mother swims away. Pups survive purely on instinct. Mother sharks provide essential nurturing, just not in the same way a wolf with pups or an eagle with chicks does.

Mother sharks help their young by giving birth to fewer, larger pups. Starting life bigger and stronger gives young sharks a better chance to survive. The number of pups in a litter depends upon the species. A lemon shark gives birth to about 12 pups every two years. Other shark species, like the sand tiger, give birth to only two pups every two years. Compare that with bony fish, which can lay millions of eggs a year.

Newborn or newly hatched sharks arrive into the world as miniature adults. (Bony fish often start life as microscopic larvae.) They have a mouth full of sharp teeth and are ready to hunt. Some pups have eaten, even hunted, before they were born. How?

While pregnant, great white mothers produce additional unfertilized eggs for their embryos to eat. The extra nutrients help the embryos grow larger and stronger. How large? A 16-foot (5-m)-long great white gives birth to 3.6- to 5.4-foot (1.1- to 1.6-m)-long pups. Some newborn great white pups are as long as a 13-year-old kid is tall!

For some pups, life's adventures begin and end before birth. Twelve or so fertilized eggs start inside a female sand tiger shark's womb. By the time the embryo is 6.5 inches (16.5 cm) long, it already has teeth. When the largest embryo absorbs all the nutrients from its yolk sac, the hungry baby looks for

A GREAT WHITE SHARK MIGHT PRODUCE ONLY FOUR TO SIX SMALL LITTERS IN HER ENTIRE LIFE.

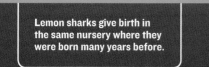
Lemon sharks give birth in the same nursery where they were born many years before.

How many sharks, rays, and human tourists can you see from this drone's-eye view?

>> ANIMAL RESCUE!

SHARK DRONES

Biologist Johann Mourier likes to count sharks. Unfortunately, counting sharks isn't as simple as floating in one spot and keeping track of sharks that pass by. Sharks move and hide—and our human eyes and swimming skills just cannot keep up, especially in shallow waters. When counting sharks underwater doesn't work, why not take to the air? That's just what Mourier and his team decided to do. The biologist developed a new way to count sharks using an unmanned aerial vehicle (UAV), which is a small remote-controlled plane often called a drone.

Getting good shark population numbers is critical for conservation. Too often, this missing vital data blocks conservation measures from being adopted. Without hard data that provides baseline numbers or evidence of declines in shark populations, governments often hesitate to adopt appropriate measures that could help save sharks. Finding new and creative ways to fill in the missing number gaps could save sharks all over the world.

Mourier discovered that flying the UAV about 40 feet (12 m) above the water was the perfect height from which to view sharks. That's like looking down from a four-story building. From that altitude, he could identify the actual species of shark or ray.

During a three-day shark count, the UAV flew back and forth over the sea, creating an imaginary checkerboard pattern. Mourier was able to recognize and count several blacktip reef sharks, rays, and even sea turtles!

Mourier hopes this is just the beginning of taking to the skies to count sharks around the world.

The mangrove forest in Bimini, Bahamas, provides a safe haven for lemon shark pups to grow up.

food—inside the female. Throughout the rest of the gestation, the largest or perhaps toughest unborn shark eats all the other embryos. By the time it's born, the pup is 3.3 feet (1 m) long and is nearly half the size of its 8-foot (2.4-m)-long mother.

Competing with, even killing, siblings is not unique to sharks. In the animal kingdom, competition to survive starts from day one. Young eagles, hyenas, penguins, and many others aggressively compete with siblings for available food. The loser often dies or is killed.

BAHAMA BABY

All over the world, shark nurseries provide a safe place for pups to grow up. Biologists know very little about the locations of most nurseries; however, they've extensively studied the lemon shark nursery in the Bahamas for decades. At this nursery, a mangrove forest blends with the ocean, creating an oasis above and below the water. The woody roots create a tangled maze through the shallow water where pups can hide and hunt.

The shallow, nearshore nursery means there is plenty of small prey to eat—like crabs, shrimp, octopuses, and small bony fish—and fewer large predators. As the young sharks grow, they start to explore farther away from the shallow water. Eventually, their hunting ground expands into the sea grass, coral, and deeper water.

When the lemon sharks are about five years old, they leave the nursery and head out to sea. The male sharks never return. Scientists in Bimini, Bahamas, recently made a big discovery about female lemon sharks. They found that they return to their birth nursery about 17 years later to give birth to their own pups.

BABY BLUES

Not all shark nurseries are near shore. Biologists recently discovered a blue shark nursery in the middle of the North Atlantic Ocean. The young sharks stay in the nursery area for about two years or until they've tripled in size. Then they leave the nursery to migrate with other blue sharks of the same age and sex.

SHARK NEIGHBORS

Many people fear sharks, yet many animals spend their days swimming among sharks without a care.

Beneath the waves, the sea bustles with life like a city full of people passing each other on the sidewalk.

Pilotfish swim with sharks. They don't pilot or direct as much as take advantage of bits of food from a shark's meal.

As if traveling on a sharp-toothed cruise ship, a remora gets a free ride and meals from the host shark.

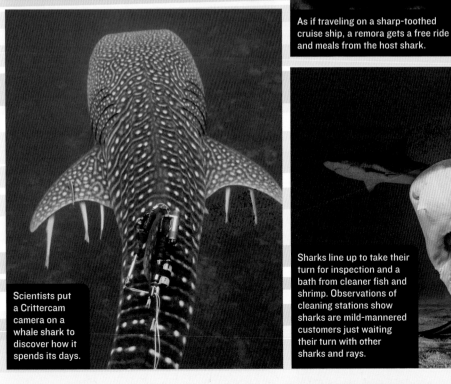

Scientists put a Crittercam camera on a whale shark to discover how it spends its days.

Sharks line up to take their turn for inspection and a bath from cleaner fish and shrimp. Observations of cleaning stations show sharks are mild-mannered customers just waiting their turn with other sharks and rays.

Why blue sharks choose that location for a nursery is still a mystery. Is it safer from larger predators than other spots in the middle of the ocean? Is there an easy food source? Do other blue sharks in different parts of the world have nurseries in the high seas? Biologists do not know yet. What they do know, however, is that even in the middle of the ocean, this nursery needs to remain a safe haven for blue sharks.

DEEP-SEA CRADLE

Recently, scientists discovered a blackmouth catshark nursery in the Mingulay Reef off the coast of Scotland. Catsharks hatch from eggs. It turns out the females lay their eggs in deep-sea corals hundreds of feet below the surface. The corals provide protection from predators. Other sharks use this area as a nursery, too, including the critically endangered spurdog and the lesser spotted dogfish. Fortunately, Scotland has designated this location as a marine protected area, helping to keep the catshark nursery safe for the baby sharks.

GROWING UP TAKES TIME

Sharks grow slowly. On average, a lemon shark grows 0.2 inch (0.5 cm) a year—less than the width of your fingernail. Compare that with people: A human baby grows 10 inches (25.4 cm) in one year! Then, children continue to grow an average of 2 to 2.5 inches (5 to 6.4 cm) a year for the next decade.

Unlike many bony fish, sharks often take a long time to grow up. Though little is known about shark growth rates, experts estimate that most do not mature until they're in their late teens or older. Long-lived sharks, like whale sharks, might not reach breeding age until their late 20s.

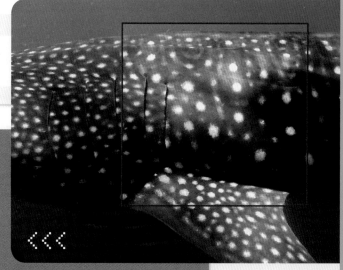

‹‹‹

>> ANIMAL RESCUE!

WILDBOOK FOR WHALE SHARKS

Jason Holmberg's life changed forever after seeing his first whale shark during a dive trip off the coast of Africa. Enchanted by the species, Holmberg soon volunteered to help scientists tag whale sharks. That's when he discovered that identifying and tracking the most recognizable fish in the world isn't all that easy. Limited data hampered whale shark conservation efforts. Holmberg knew divers and scientists had whale shark photographs from all over the world. He wondered if there was a way to use the photos and the shark's prominent spots to identify individuals.

Using his computer science background, Holmberg collaborated with an astrophysicist and a whale shark biologist. Combining their talents, the team created a pattern-recognition program adapted from software designed to map star coordinates. Turns out whale sharks' patterns are as unique as our fingerprints! Soon Wildbook for Whale Sharks was online, identifying and tracking whale sharks from photographs submitted by citizen scientists and researchers from every corner of the Earth. In the last ten years, they've collected an incredible 53,000 photos!

The program is such a success that the team expanded its identification and tracking data management system to include manta rays (a shark cousin) and even polar bears!

Check out the Wildbook at whaleshark.org.

My favorite moment in the field was when I did a night dive in the middle of more than 500 gray reef sharks that were chasing fish in between my fins. In these moments, you balance between excitement, fascination, and fear. You feel very small, but you just have to enjoy the beauty and power of nature.

>> EXPLORER INTERVIEW

DR. JOHANN MOURIER

BORN: LYON, FRANCE
JOB TITLE: RESEARCHER AT CENTER OF ISLAND RESEARCH AND ENVIRONMENTAL OBSERVATORY (CRIOBE)
JOB LOCATION: FRANCE AND FRENCH POLYNESIA
YEARS WORKING WITH SHARKS: 10

Marine biologist Johann Mourier releases a lemon shark pup.

How are you helping to save sharks?
I help save sharks by learning more about the ecology and organization of their populations. This information can help scientists evaluate their conservation vulnerabilities and in turn help us understand how to protect them.

What is the role of technology in shark conservation?
The most important technology should be noninvasive or the least invasive as possible for sharks. We can use remote technology to survey habitats, like drones that can help count sharks from the air or robots that can follow sharks. Or we can use low-invasive sampling techniques such as skin sampling in order to use it for genetic analysis or stable isotope analysis, which are both nonlethal techniques helping to acquire knowledge on shark behavioral ecology.

Best thing about working in the field?
The chance to share moments underwater with sharks. I spend a lot of time diving with sharks and taking data on their lives. They are now part of my social network as I am now able to recognize about 300 individual sharks in Moorea [in French Polynesia]. They are like friends!

Favorite conservation success story?
When I began to dive with blacktip reef sharks in Moorea, I quickly found that I could recognize individuals by the color patterns of their fins. The patterns are as different as our fingerprints. Then I realized that I always saw the same sharks together. To find out if they were family or social groups, I photographed and observed the sharks for two years and discovered that sharks formed groups of preferred "friends." It was the first study of this kind in the wild that showed sharks had friends, and it changed our view of how sharks interact.

How can kids prepare to do your job one day?
First, you have to be passionate, curious, and patient. I recommend you spend time meeting your favorite fish in an aquarium or, even better, in their natural habitat.

Some sharks, like this lemon shark, are born live.

IN THE UNITED STATES, ABOUT 96 PERCENT OF SHARKS CAUGHT RECREATIONALLY ARE RELEASED BACK INTO THE OCEAN.

A swell shark hatches from its egg case.

A SHARK PUP'S PLAYGROUND

Scientists don't know what happens to shark pups after they leave the nursery. Do they grow up at sea or find other safe locations to hunt away from larger sharks? Recently, scientists discovered two different juvenile hangouts, leading to more questions than answers.

In 2009, researchers found hundreds of juvenile whale sharks in the coral reefs of the Red Sea off the coast of Saudi Arabia. This was the first time scientists had even a hint about a whale shark nursery of any kind.

The youngsters (ranging in size from 8 to 23 feet [2.4 to 7 m] long) were about one-fifth to one-half the size of adult whale sharks. Using satellite tags, scientists discovered that the juveniles spent their days diving thousands of feet, often below 3,800 feet (1,158 m), probably in search of plankton. No adult whale sharks visited the area. Scientists wonder if it's a staging area for juveniles before they are large enough to hang out with the adults.

In 2011, Australian scientists made an exciting discovery when they identified a great white preschool. Every August to January, the coastline 30 miles (48 km) north of Sydney, Australia, becomes an underwater park for juvenile great whites. Scientists estimate the 5- to 10-foot (1.5- to 3-m)-long youngsters are no more than four years old. This stretch of paradise is a perfect fishing spot for the young sharks.

These juvenile areas provide tantalizing clues and exciting opportunities to discover more about the lost years when sharks grow up at sea.

RIO LADY

The world's largest fish, the whale shark, also hides big secrets. Recently, a whale shark named Rio Lady shared a secret with scientists.

From May to September, hundreds of whale sharks arrive in Mexico's Yucatán Peninsula. Though usually solitary, these sharks gather for the food. During this time of year, the sea becomes an all-you-can-eat plankton buffet. As many as 800 sharks spend their days sucking in the plankton-rich water and filtering out thousands of pounds of food.

Scientists take advantage of the gathering to put satellite tags on several sharks to see where the whale sharks go after they leave the area. Biologists discovered that the tagged whale sharks scattered throughout the Gulf of Mexico, Straits of Florida, and the Caribbean Sea.

But not Rio Lady. She did something completely different. Like the other whale sharks, Rio Lady traveled east through the Caribbean Sea after leaving the Yucatán plankton-fest. But then she surprised the biologists when she kept swimming all the way to the North Atlantic Ocean, eventually heading south and crossing the Equator!

When her tag fell off five months later, Rio Lady was in the middle of the South Atlantic Ocean, between the continents of South America and Africa. During those 150 days, she trekked a whopping 4,482 miles (7,213 km).

Was she heading to a nursery, a breeding area, or another plankton bloom? Scientists do not know. It's exciting to think such incredible discoveries are just waiting to happen!

THREATENED WATERS

All over the world, overfishing, construction, runoff, pollution, and other human activities affect inshore shark nurseries and future generations of sharks. For example, in the last few decades people have destroyed 30 to 50 percent of the world's mangrove forests, which are important sanctuaries for sharks and other animals.

Overfishing is especially tough on sharks. Those extra years sharks need to grow into adulthood, along with their low reproductive rates, mean it is difficult to rebuild populations devastated by continued overfishing. One species suffering from worldwide fishing is the blue shark. Every year, 20 million blue sharks die from various types of fishing.

But there is hope. People are starting to realize how important sharks are for marine ecosystems—and our entire world. Governments across the globe are recognizing the ecological significance of protecting shark nurseries and the resulting human benefits.

Mingulay Reef near Scotland is a notable example of a shark success story. In this popular recreational catch-and-release fishing area, fishermen target catsharks more than 60 percent of the time. ("Catch and release" means that after the fishermen catch the shark, they quickly release it unharmed.) Catch-and-release programs bring in $215 million for the Scottish economy. By protecting the Mingulay Reef and requiring catch-and-release fishing methods, experts estimate that the fishery could contribute as much as $15 billion to the United Kingdom's economy over the next 20 years.

Learning more about shark nurseries is an important step in shark conservation. Whether it's a shallow lagoon for lemon sharks, the middle of the ocean for blue sharks, or the catsharks' eggs hidden in deep-water coral, nurseries are vital safe havens for baby sharks. The more we know about nurseries, the better we can protect them.

Sharks, such as these vulnerable spurdog sharks, grow slowly and mature later, which adds to the challenges of rebuilding populations.

MERMAID PURSES

People call shark eggs mermaid purses, maybe because of their unusual shape. Like other animals that hatch from eggs, the baby shark gets its nutrients from the yolk. Check out some cool facts about shark eggs.

Unlike a bird's egg, which is encased in a hard shell, a shark's egg is thick and leathery with sticky tendrils to help it attach to rocks or seaweed to keep it from floating away.

The embryo wiggles inside the egg case to help circulate oxygen-rich water so it can breathe (respire).

Some shark eggs, like a horn shark's, can have a spiral shape. The color camouflages the egg case.

If an embryo inside the egg case senses a predator, it stops moving until the coast is clear.

>>RESCUE ACTIVITIES

SWIM LIKE A SHARK

Unlike well-known predators such as lions and tigers, sharks are harder to see and far more misunderstood. Perhaps more than any other animal, sharks need some help forming a positive relationship with people. Complete this rescue activity to see if you can increase the popularity of sharks at your school.

ACT

OPEN A SHARK SCHOOL

IN YOUR SHARK SCHOOL, SET UP SHARKMAKING KITS to teach people about these incredible predators. Find a place that lots of people can visit and make sure you have all the equipment you need for them to make fins and teeth, along with shark drawings and examples that will help them create their shark art.

ADVERTISE A TEETH- AND SHARK FIN–MAKING EVENT AND INVITE PEOPLE TO COME. When they arrive, explain ways they can make their own. If it gets busy, they will be able to explain your methods to other people.

MAKE AS MANY WEARABLE PIECES TOGETHER AS YOU CAN. How big can you make your school of sharks? Ask everyone to wear their fin and mask for the rest of the day.

MAKE

DRAW A DESIGNER FIN OR CREATE A MASK WITH SHARK TEETH

BRAINSTORM A SIMPLE WAY FOR PEOPLE TO WEAR MAKEABLE DORSAL FINS or a shark-toothed mask. The fin could be attached to their head, back, arm, phone, shoe, or somewhere else, and people could wear their shark mask filled with rows of sharp-looking teeth. You might think outside the box and even add your fin and teeth to something at home, like a vacuum cleaner or a car.

RESEARCH THE DIFFERENT SHAPES AND TYPES OF DORSAL FINS and shark teeth. Pick one (or more) that you think looks great.

DEVELOP AN EASY METHOD FOR PEOPLE TO MAKE THEIR OWN SHARK WEARABLES to attach to themselves or exhibit on something else. The easier your method, the more people will be able to take part.

TAKE A "SHARKIE"

TELL YOUR GUESTS ABOUT THE CHALLENGES THAT SHARKS FACE. You could do this by giving a short talk or by making and putting up some posters. It is important that you do this so they know why they are taking part and can explain it to people they meet.

CHALLENGE EVERYONE TO TAKE A SHARK SELFIE, OR "SHARKIE," WITH THE FIN OR MASK TO SHARE WITH THEIR FRIENDS. Grab a parent to share photos online. You could share your sharkie with a hashtag, such as the name of your campaign, #sharkie, or #iamashark!

ASK EVERYONE TO SIGN YOUR PETITION AND TO SHARE IT WITH OTHERS. Remember, the more signatures you get on your petition, the more effective it will be.

Here are some great things to keep in mind for your shark school:

1 Art takes many forms. Try making different types of fins, some realistic and some abstract.

2 In a visual way, give people a sense of how many teeth sharks have. You could line up toothbrushes to show how many a shark would need compared to a person over a year.

3 Create a display table with some of your "sharkies" framed to give others inspiration.

CHAPTER 4

» MARINE HUNTERS

"GREAT WHITES ARE NOT MEAN—
THEY ARE JUST WILD ANIMALS
TRYING TO SURVIVE IN A
CHALLENGING ENVIRONMENT."

—ALISON KOCK, RESEARCH MANAGER, SHARK SPOTTERS, CAPE TOWN, SOUTH AFRICA

A great white shark chomps down on a seal.

Great white sharks in False Bay, South Africa, succeed in catching seals less than 50 percent of the time.

> WHEN IT'S SUNNY, A CAPE FUR SEAL CAN SEE A SHARK ALMOST 16 FEET (5 M) AWAY. IN MOONLIGHT, IT SEES ONLY 2 FEET (0.6 M) AWAY.

Paws, claws, and teeth make tigers and polar bears fierce predators, but sharks' supremacy comes from less flashy adaptions like superior senses and artful hunting skills. With a lethal bite and supersenses, sharks are among the top predators of the sea.

ANATOMY OF AN ATTACK

A young great white shark patrols the shoreline just as the sun rises off the coast of South Africa. The 11.5-foot (3.5-m)-long shark searches for Cape fur seals using all its senses. One after the other, each sense comes into play the closer the shark gets to its prey.

The hungry shark easily hears several seals scramble into the sea from the rocky shore a couple hundred feet away. With our human hearing, the noise of the distant seals disappears in the roar of waves crashing onto rocks. To the shark, the sound of splashing or thrashing prey is like a dinner bell. It stands out from the churning water in the same way that we can recognize the distinctive tinkle of coins hitting the sidewalk on a busy street. Sharks hear prey the distance of two soccer fields away.

The great white swims toward the sound. From a distance, a shark relies on its sense of hearing and smell. Sometimes it might smell an animal first. Other times it hears it.

A seal's scent washes over the shark's nostrils. The shark follows the scent and soon the silhouette of a seal swimming at the surface comes into view. Sharks are known for their sensitive noses. A shark can detect one drop of blood in a billion drops of water. In other words, it could smell that one drop in an area the size of a backyard swimming pool.

Sharks can see movement up to 50 feet (15 m) away, but their real visual skill is seeing well in the dark. A shark sees ten times better than we do in dim light. Sharks have specially adapted eyes to hunt in the dark. Mirrorlike crystals line the back of the eye. When light enters the eye, it bounces off the "mirrors" and doubles the amount of light the eye uses to see.

The location of the eyes helps, too. Like many sharks, the great white has a nearly 360-degree view. It can see in front, to the sides, behind, above, and below. This large visual field helps when living in an

I-NSU, A SHORTFIN MAKO SHARK

In May 2013, biologists from Nova Southeastern University (NSU) in Florida, U.S.A., tagged a juvenile male shortfin mako shark off the coast of Maryland, U.S.A.

They nicknamed the five-foot (1.5-m)-long juvenile shark I-NSU after their university. When I-NSU is an adult, he'll be twice the size, about ten feet (3 m) long.

Every time I-NSU got close to the surface, the satellite tag pinged scientists, telling them where he was, like an electronic postcard.

I-NSU's travels revealed a new dimension of a juvenile mako shark's world. He tooled around the Atlantic the first year and surprised scientists by even traveling north all the way to Nova Scotia, Canada! Then, early in 2014, he started heading south, swimming all the way to Venezuela in South America. I-NSU traveled 12,000 miles (19,312 km) in just 14 months.

Before I-NSU's tag quit transmitting in July 2014, the adventurous traveler sent 350 transmissions from the northeast Atlantic, Mid-Atlantic Ridge, South America, North Carolina, Maryland, and New York.

ecosystem where predators or prey can be anywhere.

The shark lingers just deep enough to remain concealed from the oncoming seal. Through trial and error, it has learned to stalk seals at least 22 feet (7 m) down in the shadows, just out of the sunlight.

Sharks rely on two additional senses to track their prey's approach. A moving animal creates small ripples in the water that a shark can feel. A shark has lateral lines that run down each side of its body and on its head. The lateral lines are fluid-filled canals with tiny sensory hairs that feel movement in the water. A shark can feel the flutter of a swimming animal one to two body lengths away.

At the last moment of a hunt, one more sense comes into play. Sharks have electroreceptors called ampullae of Lorenzini. These electroreceptors cover the head and snout. These receptors locate electrical fields created by living animals. Think of them as sort of like metal detectors. Only instead of detecting metal, they detect prey.

In a burst of speed, the great white shark rockets through the water. Swimming 36 feet a second (11 m/s), it reaches the seal in 2.5 seconds.

The fur seal has a tenth of a second to react. If it is not killed or badly injured during the first strike, the quick and agile seal may have a chance to get away.

The shark is successful this time. With its mouth wide open, exposing several hundred teeth, the shark rams the seal with such force that both burst from the water and fly several feet into the air before crashing back into the sea. Dinnertime!

EATING MACHINES?

Some people think sharks are eating machines, gorging themselves on everything they see. Sharks eat surprisingly little food. Marine mammals such as seals and killer whales eat more than sharks of a similar size. Even you eat more than a shark that's the same size as you!

A shark can go days, even weeks, between meals. On average a shark eats only about 3 percent of its body weight a day. The calorie-rich seal blubber provides a lot of energy. If a 2,000-pound (907-kg) white shark eats about 66 pounds (30 kg) of blubber, the predator won't need to eat again for more than 11 days. Compare that to an adult killer whale, which eats about 375 pounds (170 kg) of food a day!

Electroreceptors called ampullae of Lorenzini cover the head and snout of this nurse shark.

>> ANIMAL RESCUE!

SUSTAINABLE AND SAFE SEAFOOD

Canned tuna, fish sticks, fish and chips, frozen shrimp, fresh salmon—you love it all. But how can you tell if your favorite seafood is shark safe? Look for the blue Marine Stewardship Council (MSC) eco-label on the package. MSC helps consumers navigate the ever changing, and sometimes confusing, options when trying to purchase environmentally friendly seafood.

In 1996, MSC created the first certification and labeling program recognizing and rewarding sustainable fishing techniques. MSC sets standards and works with fisheries, scientists, countries, and businesses throughout the world to change, promote, and support sustainable fishing practices.

If you eat sustainable seafood, it means you're eating seafood caught following guidelines that encourage a balance of what people need and what the species or ecosystem needs to stay healthy. For example, sustainable fisheries set catch limits to avoid overfishing a species or region. It also means targeting species or populations that are plentiful and avoiding struggling species. Sustainable fishing also means following environmentally safe fishing practices for all species in an area, including monitoring bycatch, which is a danger to sharks everywhere. More than 23,000 seafood products throughout the world are from certified sustainable fisheries. Keeping the ocean in balance means healthy environments for everyone. Eating sustainably caught food is one way you can help sharks.

Want to help your family put sustainable seafood on the table? Check out the sustainable seafood product finder at msc.org/where-to-buy/product-finder.

>> SHARK SPOTLIGHT

SUPERSENSES

Sharks can see, hear, smell, and feel movement in the water—making them awesome predators.

A shark can smell blood a half mile (1 km) away. If you could do that, you could smell baking cookies eight soccer fields away.

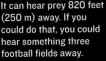

It can hear prey 820 feet (250 m) away. If you could do that, you could hear something three football fields away.

ON THE HUNT

Shark hunting styles are as distinct as the more than 500 species of sharks. One of the most feared and misunderstood hunters is the great white shark. Their size and seasonal nearshore hunting of seals and sea lions brings them close to people. Great whites became infamous because of the bloodthirsty portrayal of sharks in the movie *Jaws*. In actuality, great white sharks usually leave people alone. According to great white expert Alison Kock, "Sharks are perfectly designed by nature to catch and kill their seal and fish prey quickly and efficiently to reduce suffering."

Not all sharks eat seals or stalk prey like great whites do. Whale sharks, basking sharks, and megamouth sharks eat plankton, tiny plants and animals. Moving slower than you walk, a basking shark swims through clouds of plankton with its giant mouth open. It filters 2,000 gallons (7,571 L) of water an hour. Specialized gills filter, or trap, tons of plankton as the water passes over the shark's gills and out its gill slits.

Hammerheads use their ampullae of Lorenzini to find prey hiding beneath the sand. Some sharks, such as the mako shark, pursue fast prey. Other sharks lure prey rather than chase them. The carpet shark sits on the ocean floor and waits for prey. The fringes decorating the ornate carpet shark's mouth look like worms or bits of seaweed. A small fish swims up thinking it has discovered a dining jackpot, but becomes dinner instead. Sometimes sand tiger sharks work together to herd fish toward the beach. Trapped between the sharks and shore, the fish are easier to catch.

Whether they stalk, ambush, chase, or trick their prey, sharks use their superb senses to hunt for their all-important next meal.

BALANCING ACT

In the battle for survival between predators and prey, there's never an easy win. Even for the great white. Sharks hunting for Cape fur seals off the coast of South Africa succeed less than 50 percent of the time. Older, more experienced sharks succeed a little more often.

(continued on page 73)

With its lateral line, a shark can feel a moving animal one to two body lengths away. If you could do that, you could feel someone quietly dancing behind you without looking.

Not only can a shark see movement up to 50 feet (15 m) away, it can see ten times better than we can in dim light. If you could do that, you'd be able to see something moving across a dark basketball court.

A shark detects hidden animals from 20 inches (51 cm) away. If you could do that, you'd be able to sense a hidden animal about two footballs (or eight tennis balls) away.

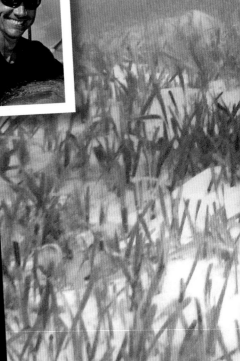

>> EXPLORER INTERVIEW

DR. DEAN GRUBBS

BORN: PERRY, FLORIDA, U.S.A.
JOB TITLE: ASSOCIATE DIRECTOR OF RESEARCH, FLORIDA STATE UNIVERSITY COASTAL AND MARINE LABORATORY
JOB LOCATION: ST. TERESA, FLORIDA, U.S.A.
YEARS WORKING WITH SHARKS: 25

How are you helping to save sharks?

I conduct scientific research that answers questions about the biology of coastal and deep-sea sharks and rays and their roles in marine eco-systems. I concentrate on species that are imperiled and poorly studied.

Favorite thing about your job?

I get to study sharks, animals that have intrigued me since childhood. In any given year I work with at least 1,500 sharks and rays from more than 50 species, including the critically endangered smalltooth saw-fish and a variety of deep-sea sharks few people have ever seen.

What is the goal of your research?

The primary goal of my research is to fill in gaps in our knowledge of the biology of sharks and rays and their roles in marine ecosystems. This information helps us sustain-ably manage populations and promote conservation and recovery of declining or endangered species. People often describe sharks as apex predators, but in truth very few shark species are top predators. Most shark species are in the middle of the food chain. These smaller sharks and rays, particularly the deep-sea species, are often neglected in research, even though they are frequently of greatest management concern.

Best thing about working in the field?

The best thing about being at sea is the excitement of not knowing what will happen next or what we may catch next. In our deep-sea surveys, we often fish for sharks more than 5,000 feet (1,524 m) deep and we never know when we will catch a species we haven't seen before or even a species that is new to science.

How can kids prepare to do your job one day?

If you want to become a marine biologist, it is critical that you do well in school so you can get into a good biology or zoology program in college. Obviously, you need to do well in science classes, but many students don't realize marine biologists spend a lot of time writing and doing math. So you need to do well in English and math courses as well.

MEMORABLE MOMENT

In 2005, I caught my first bluntnose six-gill shark, a 12-foot (3.7-m)-long female, about 1,000 feet (305 m) deep off the coast of Hawaii, U.S.A. The sixgill shark's lineage dates back 200 million years, so as a young biologist, catching one of these was on the same level as seeing a living dinosaur. After bringing her to the surface and then measuring and tagging her, I had to get in the water to watch her swim away when released. What a thrill! Since that time, I have caught more than 60 sixgills, and I still am thrilled each time I see one.

Marine biologist Dean Grubbs swims next to a tiger shark.

A high school student discovers first-hand what it's like to study sharks.

SHARK SCIENCE CLUB <<<

"No one should hate sharks," said 15-year-old Yoiidia Torres. Yoiidia and her school's marine science club spent the day with marine biologist Derek Burkholder, of the Nova Southeastern University Guy Harvey Research Institute in Fort Lauderdale, Florida, U.S.A. At the institute, kids of all ages discover firsthand what it's like to be a shark scientist.

Burkholder, the crew, and students caught sharks using specially designed equipment that won't hurt the animals. Throughout this trip, the team brought up sandbar, nurse, and other sharks.

Once a shark was secure alongside the boat, the students carefully took measurements and photographs and collected tissue, DNA, and other samples before attaching an orange identification tag to the shark. If this shark is caught or seen in the future, knowing when and where it was originally tagged can provide scientists with vital information about its movement, distribution, age, growth, and other clues.

Burkholder and the crew released each shark, alive and well, back into the water.

Fifteen-year-old Kimberly Fradley said, "What scientists are doing is really important, and they need to keep on doing it until sharks are not in danger anymore."

The sharks tagged today by the students will become part of the vital conservation efforts under way along the Atlantic coast.

IT WOULD TAKE MORE THAN EIGHT LARGE GREAT WHITE SHARKS TO EQUAL THE WEIGHT OF ONE WHALE SHARK.

Even with all of these amazing adaptations, for every trick a shark has, its prey has an equally remarkable set of adaptations and skills it uses as a defense against predators including camouflage, spines, power, and speed. The Moses sole, a kind of flatfish, secretes a bitter toxic substance that repels sharks. The hagfish, a deep-sea fish, releases slime when caught. As the shark gags on the slime clogging its gills, it instantly releases the hagfish.

Sharks, like all predators, often search for prey that is young, old, ill, or injured. Hunting equal-size prey of similar capability is a waste of energy, and likely to get the predator hurt. A healthy adult male Cape fur seal weighs nearly 800 pounds (363 kg)—and can cause serious injury to a great white shark. Like most sharks, great whites prefer to hunt smaller or weaker seals that are easier to catch and thereby require less energy to hunt.

Sharks easily become prey, too. Imagine wandering through the grocery store, concentrating on what you might eat. Just as you reach for your favorite food, BAM! You become dinner instead! This is a reality for most sharks. Some predators of sharks include bigger sharks, whales, sea lions, other fish—and even seabirds.

UNEVEN NUMBERS

Sharks play a critical role in balancing marine and nearshore ecosystems. They keep prey populations healthy by weeding out weaker animals. Without predators, the prey population in any ecosystem can multiply unchecked—with potentially devastating consequences. The ever growing prey population devours even more food. Many plants and animals cannot reproduce fast enough to satisfy an expanding—and hungry—population.

Recent studies have also shown that the existence of predators helps the environment in another way. With the threat of lurking predators, prey will carefully choose their feeding locations, feed in different areas, or target other food. For example, in Shark Bay, Australia, dugongs, a cousin of the manatee,

BIG BITE

It takes more than teeth to make a shark's bite lethal. Lacking hands or paws to grasp or hold prey, a shark's mouth is a complete multitasking tool kit.

Just as you move your hand back and forth to cut with a knife, many sharks fiercely shake their head back and forth to help teeth slice.

A smooth dogfish's flat teeth crack open crabs, lobsters, and mollusks like a nutcracker.

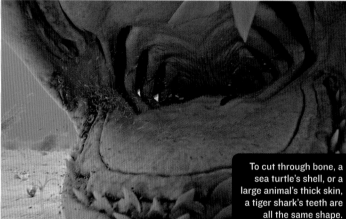

To cut through bone, a sea turtle's shell, or a large animal's thick skin, a tiger shark's teeth are all the same shape.

Sharks' teeth are like all-purpose tools. Depending on what the shark eats, the teeth might work like a knife, a hole punch, a nutcracker, a chisel, or a saw.

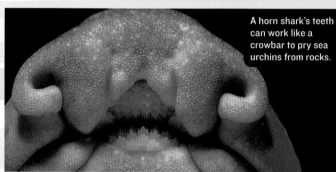

A horn shark's teeth can work like a crowbar to pry sea urchins from rocks.

A whitespotted bamboo shark can change the angle of its teeth. It can rip and tear soft prey and can also fold its teeth back, creating flat plates to smash open the prey.

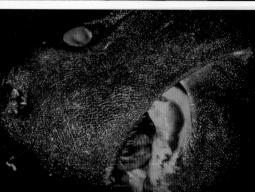

The kitefin shark's bottom row of teeth overlaps and creates a continuous cutting edge like a saw, great for eating other sharks and rays.

graze on sea grass. If tiger sharks are in the area, dugongs will feed in deeper waters so they can maneuver more easily to escape. If tiger sharks are not in the area, dugongs feed in shallower water. The variation in their feeding locations might allow the sea grass to grow into lush meadows, which in turn provide food and homes for other ocean animals and help create a balanced ecosystem.

Sharks play a key role across the world in many ecosystems. Removing these essential predators causes a tidal wave of problems across the entire ocean from the top to the bottom. "Sharks are part of a well-balanced ecosystem," said Dean Grubbs. "If any one part of that ecosystem is removed, it can have major consequences and those consequences are often unpredictable." Conservationists and inspired kids like you can help raise awareness for sharks. Even though sharks might seem fierce, these amazing hunters need our protection, too.

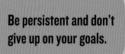

>> EXPERT TIPS

Marine biologist Dean Grubbs's tips on becoming a marine biologist:

1 Read many books about biology and the natural world in general, not only the books on sharks.

2 Be persistent and don't give up on your goals.

3 As you move ahead in your education, don't be afraid to reach out to scientists you have read about for advice. We are normal (well, sort of normal) people, too.

ANIMAL SUPERPOWERS
WHY SHARKS DON'T SHARE

HE'D SMELL IT, HEAR IT, AND SEE IT BEFORE YOU.

A SHARK NEVER HAS TO PAY.

HE EATS IT IN ONE GULP.

>> RESCUE ACTIVITIES

PLAY SHARKS AND MINNOWS WITH A TWIST

For many people, the idea of swimming with sharks is frightening. However, for the most part, sharks stay away from people. This rescue activity reimagines a popular swimming game called shark that some kids like to play in the water and even on land.

ACT

ORGANIZE A SHARK CHAMPIONSHIP

FIND A GREAT VENUE IN A PUBLIC PLACE TO HOLD A CHAMPIONSHIP MATCH OF YOUR REINVENTED GAME. If you need to, get permission to use the venue. Plan how you will use the space. Think about where the audience will watch, how many teams can play, and if you need any food, drink, music, or other supplies.

INVITE INDIVIDUALS OR TEAMS TO ENTER YOUR SHARK CHAMPIONSHIP. Consider having a prize to attract people to attend. As this is a new game, make sure you make a small rule book and have a referee whose decision is always final.

RUN THE GAME AND SEE WHO WINS THE CHAMPIONSHIP!

MAKE

REMAKE A GAME

HAVE YOU EVER PLAYED THE GAME SHARK IN THE SWIMMING POOL BEFORE? Players must swim across the pool (sometimes played while running through a forest or a field) without being tagged by someone who is the "shark."

RETHINK THE GAME SO THAT IT BETTER REFLECTS REALITY. What aims and rules can you create that will reveal who should really be chasing who? Would it be a person chasing a shark?

TRY OUT DIFFERENT RULES, SUCH AS SWITCHING THE ROLES OF PREDATOR AND PREY. Make the game as enjoyable as you can, but make sure that it also tells the story of the challenges that sharks face.

SHARE SHARK PROBLEMS

USE THE GAME AS AN OPPORTUNITY TO TELL PEOPLE WHY SO MANY SHARKS ARE VULNERABLE, threatened, and even endangered. The best way to do this is by giving a short talk at the beginning or end of the game. You could also provide information on tickets or posters.

AMPLIFY YOUR MESSAGE BY INVITING PEOPLE WITH LARGE NETWORKS OF PEOPLE TO YOUR EVENT. A network includes all of the people that a person is connected to. They could be connected to lots of people on social media as well, including Twitter, Facebook, Instagram, or by being a blogger or journalist.

ASK EVERYONE WHO ATTENDS TO SIGN YOUR PETITION. Remember, the more people who sign your petition, the more powerful it will be.

Here are some tips to reinvent a game:

1 A game is an activity people do for pleasure that has rules. You can decide on the rules of your game.

2 Changing the size of a game is a quick and easy way to reinvent a game. Try playing with a different number of people, amount of time, and space.

3 In a traditional game of shark, it is a sole shark that chases lots of people. Try inverting these roles and turning the game around.

PLAY SHARKS IN THE PARK !!
Pottery field from 10am. Bring a team of 6
Awesome prizes for the winners
SAVE THE SHARKS!!
PLAY SHARKS!!
LOVE SHARKS !!

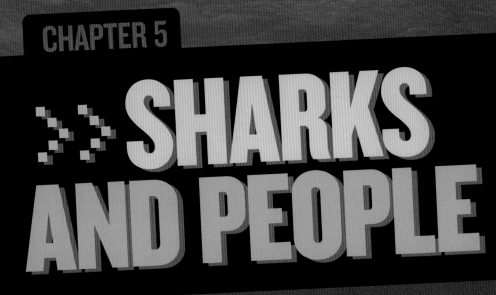

CHAPTER 5

>> SHARKS AND PEOPLE

"SHARKS MAY NOT MATTER TO YOUR LIFE, YOU THINK, BUT THEY DO."
—BRIAN SKERRY, NATIONAL GEOGRAPHIC PHOTOGRAPHER

It is said that Mana, an ancestor of the Yolngu people of the Northern Territory of Australia, took the form of a shark. While he slept on the beach, a member of a different clan speared him. Mana became so enraged, he chewed his way inland, carving and gouging out rivers and leaving behind his teeth along the way. The teeth transformed into the pandanus trees, which have shark-tooth-shaped leaves, found today along Australia's riverbanks.

ADMIRABLE ANCESTORS

Sharks hold special significance in cultures around the world. Sharks have been an important part of the culture, rituals, identity, and daily life of the Yolngu people of Australia throughout their long history. Maori, indigenous people of New Zealand, also proudly compare themselves to sharks. Both cultures value the shark's ability to survive, and they see the animal as a symbol of bravery and fearlessness.

Other island and coastal cultures around the world share this feeling. For centuries, sharks have been revered as ancestors, creators, or guardians. Legends, songs, dances, totems, and art honored sharks and told of their physical and spiritual bravery. Jewelry and knives were made from their teeth. These cultures also have relied on sharks for food.

Yet aside from cultures that depend on the ocean, throughout most of human history people knew little or nothing about sharks. Prior to coming to the Americas, Europeans didn't even have a word for shark. The word "shark" appears for the first time in a book about whales printed in the 1500s. The word is derived from the Maya word for shark, which is *xoc*. But even after being named, sharks remained under the radar for most Westerners for several more centuries.

HUNTER OR HUNTED

Before the movie *Jaws* hit the silver screen in the 1970s, most people didn't fear or even think about shark attacks. Since then, however, the media has continued to churn out sensationalized stories of shark attacks that fuel the public's fear and fascination.

TODAY, MAORI PEOPLE REPRESENT ABOUT 14 PERCENT OF NEW ZEALAND'S POPULATION.

Coastal and island people often have a special relationship with sharks.

Dogfish fins are for sale in an Indonesian fish market (above). Though the star of the soup, shark fin has no flavor or nutritional value (right).

The truth is, sharks do not hunt people. However, we swim and play where sharks live and hunt. Sometimes we cross paths. Worldwide, millions of people swim at the beach, yet there are only about 100 bites from sharks each year. Out of those 100, only 5 to 15 might result in human death. Now turn the tables and compare that with human-caused deaths of sharks.

Every hour, people kill about 11,000 sharks.

Most animals are threatened by pollution, global warming, and habitat destruction, but the biggest danger to sharks is overfishing. Biologists estimate that overfishing causes almost 96 percent of the threats against sharks.

SHARKS AS FOOD

People eat sharks. In some parts of the world, shark is a primary or vital food source. In other parts of the world, it is a delicacy. People eat sharks fresh, frozen, dried, salted, smoked, pickled, and processed. Some even eat fermented (rotten) and dried shark meat. People eat the fins, skin, liver, heart, stomach, cartilage, and even eggs.

It's not fishing or eating sharks that's the problem. It's the overfishing of sharks. As many as 100 million sharks, maybe more, die each year. Many sharks are caught for meat. Overfishing of bony fish has caused countries to begin hunting and eating more sharks, especially sharks found along the coast. Though overfishing to provide food is a problem, two bigger concerns loom over sharks: sharks accidentally taken as bycatch and shark fins taken to make shark fin soup.

SHARK FIN SOUP

As far back as the Song dynasty (A.D. 960–1279), shark fin soup has been a Chinese delicacy served at banquets to royalty and the wealthy. However, from 1949 to 1976, under the rule of Mao Zedong, the People's Republic of China prohibited the tradition.

Several things have changed in the decades since then, causing an alarming increase in the demand for shark fin soup. China opened trade with other countries and economics changed throughout many Asian countries. The custom exploded into the new era along with the increased wealth.

THE LIFE OF *JAWS*

The dorsal fin silently slices the water surface. The accompanying music, two low ominous notes, slowly repeats, matching the beat of the great white shark's tail. As the shark speeds up, the menacing music matches pace, getting louder and higher, signifying impending doom for an innocent human swimmer.

In 1975, sharks burst into popular culture, not as champions, but as boat-destroying, seashore-stalking, man-eating monsters. *Jaws*, a best-selling book by Peter Benchley, became a megahit movie that brought sharks, specifically great whites, to the attention of the average person. The fictional story depicts sharks as calculating killers, stalking and killing swimmers and boaters. Sharks went from a rarely mentioned, respected ocean creature to a bloodthirsty man-eater practically overnight.

The notion that the only good shark is a dead shark became accepted public opinion, and killing sharks was encouraged as a necessary public safety measure. Unfortunately, this contributed to the decline of shark populations along the coasts.

Fortunately, the more scientists learn and share about sharks, the more people see a different side to these incredible animals. This changing attitude is slowly turning fear into respect. An important conservation measure for saving sharks!

A model shark starred in the fictional movie *Jaws*.

Though the fin has no flavor or nutritional value, people's demand for shark fins grew. Once only for royals, shark fin soup became available to the masses. To many Asian cultures the soup embodies prosperity, and it also conveys respect and honor to guests at weddings, celebrations, holidays, even business and political dinners. Sadly, this sign of human success signifies death for sharks.

The shark fin industry is one of the world's most economically valuable seafood commodities. In other words, people all over the world, not just in Asian countries, make a lot of money buying and selling shark fins. It is a multibillion-dollar industry.

The shark fin industry is also one of the world's most ecologically expensive and damaging practices. Fin fishermen kill millions of sharks every year just for shark fin soup. Often the sharks are "processed" at sea. This process, called finning, means the fins are cut off—pectoral, dorsal, pelvic, anal, and caudal (tail)—and the shark, dead or alive, is dumped back into the sea. Of course, a shark cannot survive without its fins.

There may be some good news, though. As people and organizations around the world voice their opinion against finning, many countries have banned the practice and the import and export of shark fins. Recent reports suggest that shark fin sales might be dropping. If that trend continues, scientists and conservationists hope that the devastated shark populations, including hammerhead, mako, whitetip, and tiger sharks, might begin to rebound.

As a practice, finning is not sustainable. Finning is also wasteful, cruel, and unnecessary. It impacts populations, habitats, and the overall health of the ocean—thus the overall health of the Earth.

FISHING'S ACCIDENTAL CONSEQUENCES

Many sharks unfortunately die as unintended bycatch in commercial and recreational fishing endeavors throughout the world. Bycatch refers to nontargeted species, like sharks, caught unintentionally with the targeted species, like tuna. Nets or fishing hooks don't distinguish between sharks and tuna, or swordfish, shrimp, crabs, or other species fishermen are trying to catch.

Millions of sharks die accidental deaths every year by getting caught up with other species. Angel sharks, for instance, became critically endangered simply

(continued on page 89)

>> SHARK SPOTLIGHT
LEGENDARY SHARKS
Throughout history, coastal cultures treasured sharks and respected them for their bravery, power, and intelligence.

The ancestral shark Mana is painted on a coffin by the Yolngu Aboriginal people of Australia for safe passage.

In the Cook Islands, people used a shark-skin-covered drum in special ceremonies and to proclaim peace.

SHARK SANCTUARY

In 2009, the world's first shark haven was born! The Pacific island nation of Palau became the world's first shark sanctuary by banning commercial shark fishing in its waters. The people of Palau realized that healthy shark populations not only maintain healthy environments, they also provide important economic livelihoods for the people who protect them.

Then, in 2014, Palau went a step further and banned all commercial and export fisheries and limited recreational fishing. The Palau marine sanctuary now protects 193,000 square miles (500,000 sq km) of ocean around the islands. That's about the size of the U.S. state of Texas!

Hammerhead, oceanic whitetip, leopard, and 130 other shark and ray species live or migrate through Palau's waters. More than 40,000 divers visit Palau each year to swim with the sharks. They spend important tourist money on hotels, food, equipment, and souvenirs. These dollars stimulate Palau's entire economy.

Palau now leads the way as a voice for sharks throughout the world and encourages other nations to see the environmental and economic value in creating shark havens. More and more countries are following Palau's example by creating large protected areas or making entire coastlines into a sanctuary for sharks and other ocean life. Countries depending on the sea for their livelihood now realize that protecting the sea helps ensure the vitality of their own future.

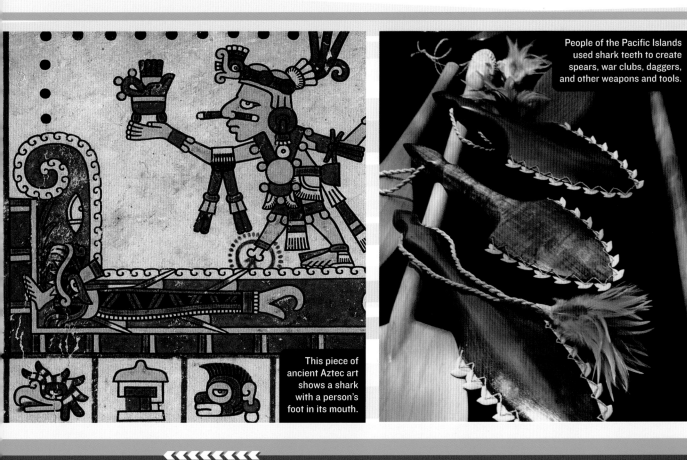

This piece of ancient Aztec art shows a shark with a person's foot in its mouth.

People of the Pacific Islands used shark teeth to create spears, war clubs, daggers, and other weapons and tools.

>> EXPLORER INTERVIEW

DR. MAHMOOD S. SHIVJI

BORN: NAIROBI, KENYA
JOB TITLE: PROFESSOR, NOVA SOUTHEASTERN UNIVERSITY HALMOS COLLEGE OF NATURAL SCIENCES & OCEANOGRAPHY; DIRECTOR, GUY HARVEY RESEARCH INSTITUTE AND SAVE OUR SEAS FOUNDATION SHARK RESEARCH CENTER
JOB LOCATION: FORT LAUDERDALE, FLORIDA, U.S.A.
YEARS WORKING WITH SHARKS: 19

Why are you doing this work?
For many reasons, but here are two main ones. First, as a biologist, how life works fascinates me, especially in the ocean, and that makes me want to study marine species. Second, sharks are amazing creatures that are also in dire need of saving because they have been overfished. My aim in studying sharks is to satisfy my curiosity about how they work, but also to contribute to information and awareness that will help conserve them.

How are you helping to save sharks?
Some countries have implemented rules to protect certain sharks. Unfortunately, once the fins are removed from the shark, identifying whether the fins are from a protected species is difficult. I developed a fast-acting genetic test that quickly identifies the shark DNA. This genetic test is so fast and easy, government law enforcement agencies use it to identify illegal trade of shark fins and prosecute offenders committing these crimes. Think of it as *CSI: Shark Fin!* The availability of this test has helped reduce the amount of illegal shark fin trade, thus helping save sharks.

Best thing about working with sharks?
On just about every field expedition, we see something unexpected and learn something new about shark behavior. These creatures never cease to amaze, and that makes me realize how much more there is to learn about them. That motivates me to do more research, including exploring their DNA to try to understand what really makes these marvelous animals tick at the most fundamental level—their genes!

What are you working on next?
Expanding the Guy Harvey Research Institute's long-term shark migration habits research. The Save Our Seas Foundation Shark Research Center is expanding our investigations at the deepest possible genetics level to understand what makes a shark a shark! We hope our discoveries will raise the public's awareness of how absolutely fascinating sharks are, and the importance of saving them.

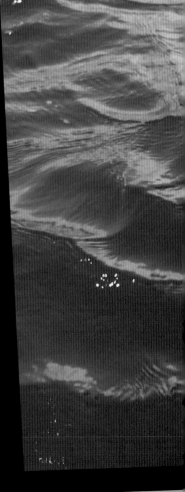

To be honest, the most memorable moment came in the lab when we first discovered using genetics that some sharks can produce babies without needing to have their eggs fertilized! This was the first discovery that sharks were capable of this type of reproduction, and it made news around the world. This discovery was certainly a "Wow!" moment, revealing yet another amazing aspect about sharks.

Shark expert Mahmood Shivji tags a shark. After measuring and collecting its DNA, he releases it from the boat side.

I'M FINISHED WITH FINS

In 2011, the nonprofit Shark Savers launched the I'm FINished With FINS campaign aimed at consumers in Hong Kong, Singapore, Malaysia, Taiwan, and mainland China, all countries where shark fin soup is a deep-rooted custom.

Consumers drive the demand for shark fins. If consumers choose not to purchase or partake in fin soup, demand drops. Less demand means fewer sharks die for their fins.

In Asian countries, serving shark fin soup at special celebrations shows honor and respect to family, friends, and special guests. Not serving or eating it might be considered disrespectful. This campaign shares conservation concerns while being mindful and respectful of traditions, culture, and social expectations.

The campaign raises awareness of the global plight of sharks and encourages people to pledge not to eat shark fin. It also provides individuals with polite and courteous ways to say "No, thank you" and share why they have made the decision not to eat shark fin soup. This grassroots effort was originally aimed at young people and promoted through various media platforms. As momentum grew, corporations, celebrities, and politicians started supporting the movement.

Shark awareness programs, like the I'm FINished With FINS campaign, are working. As consumer understanding of the conservation concerns for sharks grows, the demand for shark fins declines.

I'm FINished WITH FINS
我不翅了

éPure
MEMBRANOUS
JELLY MASQUE

89

éPure X Shark Savers FUNDRAISER FOR SHARKS

because they're scooped up in nets meant for bottom-dwelling fish, shrimp, crabs, and other seafood.

Bycatch used to be discarded (dumped back into the sea) or eaten. Unfortunately, because of the soaring price of shark fins, shark bycatch has become a lucrative business. For many nations, the bycatch of sharks is unregulated and unlimited. Even if a country passes laws to limit bycatch, the laws are often not enforced. In the middle of the ocean, sharks and other ocean animals have few safe zones.

Bycatch is sometimes unavoidable. However, it is critical to monitor and reduce bycatch mortality for the health of the ocean—and for the overall health of the planet, too. The United States is at the forefront of shark management programs. U.S. government officials are working with scientists and fishermen to continue searching for innovative ways to reduce bycatch without negatively impacting fisheries and revenue. Kids like you may have the next great idea!

HEALTHY WATERS FOR ALL

The ocean feeds the world. In order for that to continue to happen, shark populations must stay healthy. Every nation can be part of shark conservation. It will take all of our global efforts to rebuild and conserve populations of this key predator.

With the increase of deep-sea fishing, mining, and other environmental threats, countries need to conserve marine areas for sharks through internationally coordinated and enforced protection.

What about your country? Sharks need help across international waters. Spread the word about this important predator today.

>> **EXPERT TIPS**

Marine biologist Mahmood Shivji's tips on what it takes to study sharks:

1 You have to be curious and enjoy learning about the wonderful world of biology.

2 Learn all that you can about science; even find opportunities to do research in middle and high school.

3 You have to like being a science explorer. If you do, it's a really interesting job!

Sharks' lives intertwine with peoples' lives, no matter where we swim, fish, or live.

>>> RESCUE ACTIVITIES

SHARKS BY THE NUMBERS

The issues that sharks face are largely invisible. Despite many species being very large and famous, sharks are more often out of sight. It might seem obvious, but living underwater in remote places makes it harder for us to comprehend the scale of sharks' decline. The purpose of this rescue activity is to make it easier for people to visualize the problem by seeing the numbers.

ACT

GATHER DATA

RESEARCH INCREDIBLE SHARK FACTS AND THINK ABOUT HOW TO PRESENT THE DATA IN A VISUAL WAY. Watch an aquarium's live shark webcast and see how they look and behave. Sketch pictures of sharks and include them in your infographic. Scan this book for facts about the incredible senses of sharks. Also note how shark populations are declining around the world because of overfishing. Use a notebook or a computer to keep notes of the best facts you find.

SEARCH THE INTERNET TO FIND EVEN MORE FACTS that will help people to understand the scale of the problem. Make sure to do your research with reliable sources, such as scientific organizations, newspapers, and conservation groups.

MAKE

CREATE A SHARK INFOGRAPHIC

INFORMATION GRAPHICS ARE A FORM OF VISUAL STORYTELLING that will share important information, such as the number of sharks killed in a specific geographic range, what countries are doing a good job of conserving sharks, and the IUCN ranking of some shark species, from most endangered to least vulnerable.

GET FAMILIAR WITH THE INFORMATION and ask yourself questions about the data. What information is surprising or interesting? Develop a message for your audience.

MAKE IT EASY TO FOLLOW THE INFORMATION. It might look like a confusing pile, but sort through it and find the story within the information. Sometimes you don't even need to include numbers in an infographic. For example, when comparing shark teeth, it's probably best just to draw the different teeth!

DECIDE WHICH ARE THE MOST SHOCKING FACTS THAT YOU HAVE FOUND. These will probably be very large numbers. A good example is the fact that 100 million sharks are killed by people each year. What would this number of sharks look like if you were to express it in a visual way?

OVER 100 MILLION SHARKS ARE KILLED EVERY YEAR, ENOUGH TO CIRCLE THE EARTH 3X

NO SHARK FIN SOUP

NO FISHING

Here are some tips for making a great infographic:

1 An infographic can be a drawing, map, chart, graph, illustration, or even a photograph.

2 An infographic should make it easier for someone to understand something big or complicated.

3 In your infographic, compare and contrast the data to illustrate relationships and tell the story of sharks.

SHARE

PUBLISH YOUR WORK

WRITE A CAPTION FOR YOUR INFOGRAPHIC so that people understand why you have made it. Be sure to include a link to your petition so that you can collect even more names.

SHARE YOUR INFOGRAPHIC IN A PUBLIC PLACE. This could be on a wall in your school or community center. Pick a place that lots of people visit and spend time in.

GRAB AN ADULT AND CONSIDER POSTING AN IMAGE OF YOUR INFOGRAPHIC ONLINE so that people can share what you have done with other people. This will help to get your message out to an even bigger audience.

"WE NEED TO CREATE AND EMPOWER A NEW GENERATION OF SCIENTISTS AND ADVOCATES."

—RACHEL GRAHAM, FOUNDER AND EXECUTIVE DIRECTOR OF MARALLIANCE

People travel the world to get a chance to see a whale shark up close.

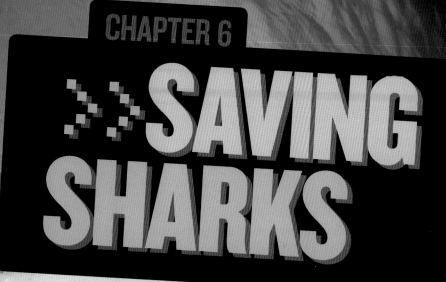

CHAPTER 6

>> SAVING SHARKS

Sharks are tough, intelligent survivors vital to ocean food webs. People all around the globe have the power to give them a voice and prevent this sleek predator from fading away.

OCEAN VIEWS

For some cultures, sharks represent courage and honor. For many countries, sharks provide a healthy diet and economy. For the world, sharks mean healthy oceans.

We protect what we love, but how do you get people to love a misunderstood predator like a shark? One way is to provide opportunities for people to learn more about sharks, to help understand and appreciate them and change the world's view of this precious predator. It's happened before with another animal people didn't care about: whales. In the 1900s, many whale species were drifting toward extinction because of overhunting. People did not know or care about the devastation until scientists vocalized their concerns. Over the next few decades, as people and scientists learned more about whales, attitudes shifted. Today, people cherish whales and fight to protect them.

Protecting sharks doesn't mean an end to fishing or eating seafood. It means carefully managing fishing practices to keep predators and prey in balance. By limiting the number of sharks taken, finding ways to reduce bycatch, and promoting ongoing research and conservation practices, we can help turn the tide for sharks.

Scientists and governments face big challenges. Sharks are elusive creatures, and data about different species populations is sparse. One reason governments have hesitated to make changes to protect sharks is our limited knowledge.

Fortunately, with the help of satellite tagging, DNA studies, and other types of technology, biologists learn something new about sharks every day.

One tool helping biologists is National Geographic's Crittercam. It is a video camera that safely and temporarily attaches to a shark's fin, giving us a shark's-eye view of life in the sea. Other researchers are testing remote-controlled robotic technology to accompany sharks on migrations and hunts. These amazing

SCIENTISTS CAN DETERMINE THE AGE OF SOME SHARKS BY THE SPINE ON THEIR DORSAL FIN.

LOGIC marine

Long-term studies, like the one in Bimini, Bahamas, just scratch the surface in our understanding of sharks and their behavior.

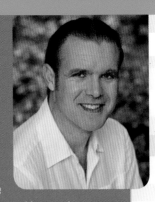

PRISTINE SEAS

In 2009, Enric Sala, director of National Geographic's Pristine Seas initiative, went back in time when he plunged into the waters near the uninhabited Line Islands in the Pacific Ocean—about 1,500 to 2,100 miles (2,414 to 3,380 km) south of Hawaii, U.S.A.

Sala and the Pristine Seas expedition team spent thousands of hours underwater documenting a world untouched by people. They found a rainbow of healthy corals carpeting the seafloor, decorated by fish, shrimp, and crabs of all shapes and sizes. They also found vibrantly colored clams the size of footballs, shark nurseries, and many curious adult sharks.

"Diving in the southern Line Islands is like getting in a time machine and traveling back to the reefs of the past, when

sharks—and not humans—were the top predators," Sala said.

Sala is on an important mission to find, explore, and protect the ocean's last few wild places, like this underwater paradise. His research expeditions also raise awareness of threatened ecosystems and encourage the restoration of habitats already impacted by people.

Pristine Seas works with global and business leaders plus local communities to create ocean sanctuaries, expand scientific research, and educate the public. The same important steps are needed to save sharks.

Pristine Seas' conservation efforts have already inspired government leaders to create five reserves throughout the world totaling more than 463,322 square miles (1.2 million sq km). In 2014, Kiribati president Anote Tong announced the closure of the southern Line Islands and the Phoenix Islands (an area about the size of California) to all commercial fisheries, ensuring that this rare paradise remains pristine.

Whether exploring pristine places or restoring threatened habitats, Pristine Seas is one more way people are helping to save sharks' homes.

gadgets open a whole new world of research and understanding of sharks' role in the sea.

SHARK SHANGRI-LA

To combat the decline in shark populations, some governments have focused their efforts on protecting sharks in their own backyards. Since 2009, many nations have created shark sanctuaries along their shores. Today these havens protect nearly five million square miles (13 million sq km) of ocean, providing sharks with safe zones free from fishing. That's an area two times the size of Mexico! These same countries are encouraging and challenging other nations to join them in the protection of sharks and fight for the health of the ocean.

Once sharks leave these protected areas, however, they're at risk. The ocean doesn't have fences or easily defined borders. Some countries have taken giant leaps in protecting sharks by working on a global level to regulate and limit the number of sharks taken in international waters.

Governments, fishermen, and biologists are also working together to limit bycatch. They are designing nets that trap the fish, shrimp, or squid, but also allow sharks an escape route. Others are trying to invent nets to discourage sharks from getting too close in the first place, sort of like an invisible fence.

In the past, sea turtles, sea otters, whales, and dolphins died after being caught as bycatch. Today, inventions and safer fishing practices help keep them safe. Turtle excluder devices (TEDs) in nets help sea turtles safely escape. It's like a trap door that the turtle can sneak out of while the fish and shrimp remain in the net.

Fishermen use purse seine nets to encircle and catch tuna. Before hauling the net on to the boat, fishermen lower the top of the net below the surface and herd out accidently caught dolphins, porpoises, and other air-breathing animals.

Though these approaches do not work as well for sharks, someday soon someone will invent the perfect shark safety net. Maybe that someone is you!

TODAY'S TECHNOLOGY

To learn more about sharks, scientists track and monitor them in a few ways.

Acoustic tags are similar to satellite tags. Rather than sending information to a satellite, special receivers placed in an underwater area pick up the signals sent by the shark's tracking device.

Scientists attach a satellite tag to a shark's dorsal fin. It tracks information such as the shark's travels and diving patterns. The data is then sent to scientists.

Shark DNA studies have expanded our understanding of populations and increased species identification. They have also helped find people illegally selling shark fins.

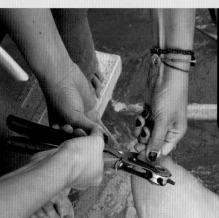

National Geographic's Crittercam attached to a dorsal fin captures a day or week in the life of a shark.

A robotic underwater vehicle can follow a shark to record its behavior, travels, and other data and then transmit that information to scientists.

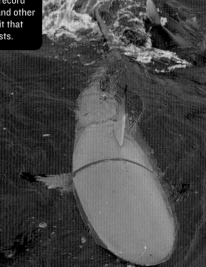

Scientists track sharks through identification tags they attach to the shark. Biologists keep a record of its size, health, and even DNA. When fishermen catch tagged sharks, they contact the scientists to share the shark's ID number.

MEEKO

Meeko, a juvenile female blue shark, swims off the coast of Nova Scotia, Canada, wearing the latest in eco-fashion, an acoustic tracking tag. During the next six years, Meeko will take scientists on a far-reaching journey into the North Atlantic.

The four-foot (1.2-m)-long, 37-pound (17-kg) shark is part of a long-term study by Dalhousie University. Blue sharks travel in groups segregated by gender and age. Scientists are studying Meeko's travels, along with those of 19 other female juvenile blue sharks, to gain important insights.

As Meeko swims throughout the North Atlantic, various acoustic receiving stations pick up her signal. Receivers placed on oil and gas rigs or anchored to the ocean floor give biologists a 3-D picture of her underwater travels.

Meeko's acoustic tag has a long life span, up to six years, giving scientists an amazing opportunity to follow her as she grows up. Not only are scientists learning about Meeko and the other blue sharks, but now 23 biology students, mentored by the scientists working on the project, have learned how to track sharks.

BACK THE SHARK FIN BAN

The shark fin industry—from fishing to the import, export, and sale of fins at stores and restaurants—is still legal in many nations. Although few people outside of Asian countries eat shark fin soup, the shark fin industry has been a worldwide effort. Until recently, most nations have participated in this commercial fishery.

Today, more than 70 countries, regional fisheries, and local governments have passed anti-finning laws, including Australia, the United States, Costa Rica, South Africa, Brazil, Oman, and others.

People hold the power for change. The people buying, selling, and eating shark fins make the industry profitable. There's hope, though: If people have the power to drive the shark fin industry, they also have the power to stop it. Citizens can raise their voices and inspire and educate others to stop serving shark fin soup. Voters can encourage their governments and fishing industries to embrace the importance of shark conservation.

(If you live where shark fin soup is served, participate in the I'm FINished With FINS campaign. See page 88.)

A CLOSER LOOK AT SHARKS

The future for sharks looks bright because of the enthusiasm of scientists, governments, and kids like you. A great way for shark conservation to gather momentum is to provide unforgettable opportunities for people to learn more about sharks, to see them up close, and even interact with them.

Many people get a chance to see sharks in new ways by visiting aquariums. Aquariums connect people and ocean animals. Seeing sharks gliding through the water among unconcerned brightly colored fish helps people see sharks in a new light.

Aquariums also gather important information. They collect data that is often hard to track in the wild, such as growth rates, food intake, and breeding and other behaviors. Aquariums support shark research and conservation efforts in the wild, too.

Some people want to get even closer to sharks. Boat tours and related shark programs, where people swim with or near sharks, have become big business. This is good news for sharks. Tourism dollars (continued on page 102)

>> **ANIMAL RESCUE!**

CREATING A SHARK SANCTUARY

What can you do in 18 months? Change the world! Just ask Jessica Cramp, scientist, surfer, diver, conservationist, and National Geographic emerging explorer.

Jessica grew up in Pennsylvania, U.S.A. Like other kids, she spent many happy hours playing in the woods, reading, and dreaming about the big adventures of scientists and explorers that she admired. All of this ignited her passion for science and nature.

After college, Cramp wanted to make an impact on the world, a goal that eventually led her to the Cook Islands, halfway between Hawaii, U.S.A., and New Zealand. There, Cramp volunteered for the newly founded Pacific Island Conservation Initiative (PICI), a local research outreach and advocacy organization. She jumped right in by starting a campaign to make the Cook Islands a shark sanctuary. She talked to local ambassadors, fishermen, and government leaders. She searched for island citizens who cared about sharks and helped other citizens realize why they should care. Eighteen months later, the Cook Islands shark sanctuary was born! It protects 771,050 square miles (2 million sq km) of ocean. That's about the size of Mexico.

Cramp isn't stopping there. She realized that creating a sanctuary is just the first step. "It's important that reserves are more than big headlines," Cramp said. "We need to support the communities we just rallied behind and encourage nations to follow through by supporting research and enforcing laws to truly conserve and protect sharks and ocean."

>> MEMORABLE MOMENT

I've had so many great moments, but two of them include being surrounded by more than 50 fast and beautiful gray reef sharks at Ras Mohammed [a national park on the Sinai Peninsula in Egypt] in the Red Sea in 1991 and spending time with Mr. Facey, an 18-foot (5.5-m) juvenile whale shark that wouldn't leave me alone. He would nudge me in the stomach and became my companion during an entire dive at Gladden Spit in Belize.

>>EXPLORER INTERVIEW

DR. RACHEL GRAHAM

BORN: WASHINGTON, D.C., U.S.A.; RAISED IN TUNIS, TUNISIA
JOB TITLE: FOUNDER AND EXECUTIVE DIRECTOR OF MARALLIANCE
JOB LOCATION: BASED IN BELIZE; ALSO TRAVELS TO SEVERAL OTHER COUNTRIES
YEARS WORKING WITH SHARKS: 18

How are you helping to save sharks?
I conduct research and monitoring of sharks that help to promote their conservation and management. This work is very broad so I also train fishers, other biologists, and rangers to undertake the monitoring. I also educate children, students, and the public to change attitudes toward sharks and rays.

Favorite part of your job?
There are many aspects of my job that I love. Being in or on the water and working with animals is exhilarating. Diving and seeing sharks swimming in the wild, catching and tracking sharks to better understand their behaviors, watching fishers who used to hunt sharks now protecting them, and seeing the fear fall away from people who encounter sharks for the first time and realize how beautiful and essential these animals are to our seas.

Best thing about being in the field?
The best thing about being in the field is simply being in or on the water and working with animals. It's exhilarating.

Worst thing about being in the field?
The long periods of waiting in small 25-foot (7.6-m) boats to catch sharks, often under a hot tropical sun and in feisty, rough seas.

What are your future plans?
Keep working with those who depend on sharks for survival and do what I can to decrease pressures on sharks and other big fish in ways that are accepted and adopted by these fishermen, tour guides, and other people.

It takes skill, speed, and several hands for marine biologist Rachel Graham and her team to gather information before releasing the shark.

good news for sharks. Tourism dollars have replaced money once earned from shark fishing in countries with shark sanctuaries. Local citizens have discovered living sharks pay for themselves. The Australian Institute of Marine Science calculated that in Cocos Island National Park in Costa Rica, a living hammerhead is worth $1.6 million over its 20-plus-year life span. More sharks mean more money for local communities and helps support shark conservation efforts, too.

START A SHARK CAMPAIGN

Everyone can step up for shark conservation. Across the world, individuals, fisheries, and governments can make a big splash. Inspired citizens can become strong advocates for these threatened species. There's no reason to wait. Your interest in this book has already shown you care about sharks. Today, a solution can start with you!

There are plenty of ways to help. Start at home. If you eat seafood, you can help sharks by choosing sustainable seafood for dinner. Encourage your local stores and restaurants to serve sustainable seafood, too. (Remember reading about sustainable seafood choices on page 68?)

Biologists discover something new about sharks all the time. Learn everything you can! Read National Geographic's magazines or follow the progress of National Geographic's Pristine Seas initiative to keep up with the latest shark and ocean news. Share what you learn with friends, family, even your teacher and classmates. By telling about sharks—shark protection measures, the latest discoveries, or just how incredible your favorite shark is—you'll help inspire others to help conserve this fantastic animal! Enthusiasm is contagious: Your love of sharks will catch on! What do you do with all that knowledge? Make a difference.

In 2011, high school students from the island of Guam took their passion to the streets. They created signs to bring awareness to the public about the plight of sharks. They participated in public hearings and petitioned legislators. Owing in part to the kids' campaign, the government of Guam became the third in the Pacific to enact laws against shark finning and the trade or sale of shark fins, proving that kids can make a really big difference. You can, too!

Just like the kids from Guam, you can contact your local and federal representatives. Encourage the creation of marine sanctuaries in your country. Let them know you support the banning of shark finning and want strong conservation measures in place to protect sharks by reducing bycatch. If you live near an ocean or stream, participate in beach cleanup days. Volunteer with scientific organizations, nature centers, zoos, or aquariums. "Create a plan of how your daily life can help sharks," said Jessica Cramp. "For example, you can reduce your carbon footprint by turning off lights, walking to school, and using reusable bags at the store."

The biggest issues facing sharks, finning and bycatch, might seem too big for one kid to change. One voice is hard to hear. But what about 1.8 billion? That's how many kids live in the world. If kids all over the Earth start shouting to save sharks, people will listen. Sharks are counting on you. Let's save the sharks!

Sharks captivate millions of kids at aquariums, creating awareness and appreciation.

KIDS MEET SHARKS

You might think being underwater and face-to-face with a shark is scary. But kids from Belize discovered it's not.

Kids can be ambassadors for shark conservation. This is especially true in countries that share their livelihoods with sharks. The Central American country of Belize has 240 miles (386 km) of prime Caribbean coastline. Yet many of Belize's children haven't even seen the ocean, let alone one of the 42 shark and ray species that live along the coast. Conservation biologist Rachel Graham decided to create a program called Kids Meet Sharks. The program gets kids in the water, face-to-face with sharks, and they discover firsthand the wonder of sharks.

Graham takes groups of elementary to high school students on these ocean excursions. By snorkeling and interacting with sharks, she sees a child's fear transform into deep appreciation. Graham's program also fosters a sense of pride in Belize's citizens for their ocean ecosystem and its animals.

After seeing sharks up close, Graham hopes the kids will become advocates, tell the world about sharks, and use their knowledge to one day help their country's conservation efforts. To learn more about Kids Meet Sharks, visit belizesharks.org.

>> RESCUE ACTIVITIES

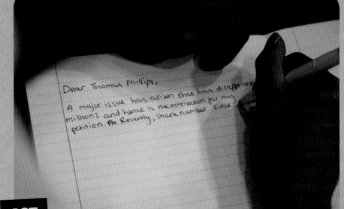

Dear Thomas Phillips,

A major issue has arisen that has disappeared millions and hence is the motivation for my petition. Recently, shark number since

SHARE YOUR PETITION

In our first rescue activity, you wrote a letter of petition. By doing each of the rescue activities at the end of each chapter in this book, you might have a number of signatures of support on your petition. The more names you collect, the stronger your petition will be, but even a single letter signed by yourself can be incredibly powerful if sent in the right way. This final rescue activity is to send your petition.

ACT

POST YOUR PETITION!

SEND YOUR PETITION TO YOUR CHOSEN DECISION-MAKER. Make sure you keep the original of your list of signatories so that you do not lose it.

EMAIL IS THE QUICKEST, EASIEST, AND CHEAPEST WAY TO SEND YOUR PETITION, but it may not be the most effective. If you can, deliver the petition by hand and ask for a meeting with the decision-maker. If this is not possible, a written letter may have more of an impact.

BE WILLING TO SEND YOUR PETITION MORE THAN ONCE. If you do not hear back from the decision-maker, keep sending the petition until you do!

MAKE

WRITE A PRESS RELEASE

DRAFT TEXT THAT YOU CAN SEND TO YOUR LOCAL OR REGIONAL MEDIA. A press release is a short story about what you have done and the reasons why. A journalist who sees the press release might decide to write a story. The more attention you can raise, the more pressure you will put on the decision-maker you are writing to.

MAKE SURE THAT YOU INCLUDE EXAMPLES, EVIDENCE, AND STATISTICS IN YOUR PRESS RELEASE. If you have photos from doing any rescue activities in this book, include them. Newspapers and websites love good photos.

ASK SOMEONE TO PROOFREAD YOUR PETITION AND PRESS RELEASE before you send it out. You will be taken more seriously if your work looks professional.

SAVE SHARKS

Take your skills and abilities further by helping sharks and other endangered species professionally. By doing well in school you could become a:

SHARE

SHARE YOUR PRESS RELEASE

RESEARCH AND MAKE A LIST OF JOURNALISTS IN YOUR LOCAL COMMUNITY. Make sure you include their name and email. Their social media handle (or name) and telephone number will also be useful.

SEND YOUR PRESS RELEASE TO THE PEOPLE ON YOUR CONTACT LIST. Ask them to include your story in your local newspaper or on a radio show. It is a good idea to follow up your email with a telephone call. A conversation may persuade them to run your story.

KEEP YOUR SUPPORTERS UPDATED ABOUT YOUR PROGRESS. If you get a reply from your chosen decision-maker, be sure to let them know the outcome. The reply you receive will determine what you do next!

1 CAMPAIGNER
Keep up the good work you have already started and run professional campaigns to protect wildlife.

2 MARINE BIOLOGIST
Study and understand sharks by observing them in the wild. You could do this by using a specialist camera, satellite system, or by consulting an expert who has experience scuba diving with sharks.

3 GEOGRAPHER
Geographers work to understand the relationships between people, wildlife, and the environment. This understanding can lead to better decision-making and the protection of wildlife and habitats.

>> CONCLUSION

A month after the divers removed the rope from Atlas's neck, he again picks up the scent of fish blood in the water. He quickly finds the boat and divers. Atlas gracefully swims near the divers and, turning around, displays his strong body and long pectoral fins. His healthy shark skin shimmers in the tropical sun.

Not only has the once dying shark gained weight, his injury is healing as if an underwater veterinarian treated him. His rescuers are thrilled about his return, and they feed him as much as they can to keep him on the road to recovery.

Throughout the rest of that diving season, Atlas comes back every day to find the boat and divers. The sight of Atlas creates a strong connection between shark-spotting tourists and these magnificent creatures in the ocean. The tourists realize how important it is to protect these vital predators—and the ocean that depends on them.

As Atlas regains his strength, he'll continue to grow larger. He won't reach maturity until he's almost 20 years old. Then Atlas will breed and help rebuild the dusky shark's vulnerable population.

During the last dive of the summer season, a bluish gray streak flashes past the divers. No longer the sluggish, injured shark the divers first met, Atlas now glides and twists through the water effortlessly. The divers admire the beauty of the shark they helped save. Atlas is now the lead in an important shark conservation story that people will share—the story of Atlas, the shark that thankfully got away!

Atlas demonstrates the resilience and fierce determination of sharks. With the right resources, along with our support and help, sharks can bounce back from today's challenges. Together we can do it. We can save sharks!

A month after divers removed the rope, Atlas is on the road to recovery.

>>RESOURCES

WANT TO LEARN MORE?
Check out these great resources to continue your mission to save sea turtles!

IN PRINT

Clark, Eugenie. *The Lady and the Sharks.* The Peppertree Press, 2010.

Doubilet, David, and Jennifer Hayes. *Face to Face With Sharks.* National Geographic Society, 2009.

Ebert, David A., Sarah Fowler, and Marc Dando. *A Pocket Guide to Sharks of the World.* Princeton University Press, 2015.

Helfman, Gene, and George H. Burgess. *Sharks: The Animal Answer Guide.* Johns Hopkins University Press, 2014.

Musgrave, Ruth A. *Everything Sharks.* National Geographic Society, 2011.

Pocket Genius: Sharks. Dorling Kindersley, 2012.

Schreiber, Anne. *National Geographic Readers: Sharks.* National Geographic Society, 2008.

ONLINE

Florida Museum of Natural History
Manages the International Shark Attack File and provides background information on shark species.
flmnh.ufl.edu/fish/sharks/sharks.htm

Guy Harvey Research Institute
Follow the travels of mako, tiger, oceanic whitetip, and other Atlantic sharks monitored by satellite transmitters.
cnso.nova.edu/ghri

National Geographic Channel
Take an expedition with a research team in this game to measure the catch, tag it with a GPS tracking device, and take a blood sample.
channel.nationalgeographic.com/wild/shark-attack
-experiment-live/interactives/expedition-great-white

National Geographic Education
Check out everything National Geographic Education has to offer about sharks, from lesson plans to cool activities, and more.
education.nationalgeographic.com/education/topics/sharks/

National Geographic Kids
Creature feature provides information on animals from around the world.
kids.nationalgeographic.com

Save Our Seas Foundation
Supports and reports on shark research and conservation efforts throughout the world.
saveourseas.com

Sharks4Kids
A collection of shark resources, including videos, news, and more, for kids and teachers.
sharks4kids.com

WATCH

"Crittercam POV: 'Swim' With Gray Reef Sharks."
video.nationalgeographic.com/video/crittercam/
crittercam-grey-reef-shark

"Shark Alert! Species Struggle."
video.nationalgeographic.com/video/news/wild-chronicles/
sharks-wcvin?source=relatedvideo

"Tiger Sharks vs. Turtles."
video.nationalgeographic.com/video/crittercam/
shark_tiger_turtles

video.nationalgeographic.com/search?subject=animals/
fish/sharks

PLACES TO SEE SHARKS AROUND THE WORLD

Georgia Aquarium, Atlanta, Georgia, U.S.A.
georgiaaquarium.org

Monterey Bay Aquarium, Monterey, California, U.S.A.
montereybayaquarium.org

National Aquarium, Baltimore, Maryland, U.S.A.
aqua.org

Oregon Coast Aquarium, Newport, Oregon, U.S.A.
aquarium.org

SeaWorld, Inc., San Antonio, Texas U.S.A.
seaworld.org

Shedd Aquarium, Chicago, Illinois, U.S.A.
sheddaquarium.org

Vancouver Aquarium Marine Science Centre,
Vancouver, British Columbia, Canada
vanaqua.org

Ocean Park, Aberdeen, Hong Kong
oceanpark.com.hk

Find a shark near you. Visit the Association of
Zoos and Aquariums website: aza.org.

ORGANIZATIONS IN THIS BOOK

I'm FINished With FINS
For more information, check out page 88
finishedwithfins.org

International Union for Conservation of Nature
For more information, check out pages 42–43
iucn.org/

Manx Basking Shark Watch
For more information, check out page 41
manxbaskingsharkwatch.org

MarAlliance
For more information, check out page 101
maralliance.org

Marine Stewardship Council
For more information, check out page 68
msc.org

Nova Southeastern University Oceanographic Center
For more information, check out page 86
cnso.nova.edu

Wildbook for Whale Sharks
For more information, check out page 53
whaleshark.org

SPECIAL EVENTS

FINTASTIC FRIDAY:
Giving Sharks, Skates, and Rays a Voice

Everyone needs a special day, including sharks! WhaleTimes, a nonprofit marine science organization—whose director, Ruth A. Musgrave, is the author of this book—created Fintastic Friday, a holiday for sharks and some of their cousins, skates and rays.

Mark your calendar to be sure you celebrate sharks with a holiday you can sink your teeth into the second Friday in May! Check out the organization at **whaletimes.org.**

Boldface indicates illustrations.

> > IMAGE CREDITS

From page 7: $10.00 donation to National Geographic Society. Charges will appear on your wireless bill or be deducted from your prepaid balance. All purchases must be authorized by account holder. Must be 18 years of age or have parental permission to participate. Message and data rates may apply. Text STOP to 50555 to STOP. Text HELP to 50555 for HELP. Full terms: www.mGive.org/T

CREDITS

Dedication
To Ays, Ampy, DD, Dash, and all my land-shark friends —Ruth A. Musgrave
To all sharks —Daniel Raven-Ellison

Special Thanks
Thank you to all my friends at National Geographic Kids Books for including sharks in a beautiful series that raises awareness and encourages compassion.

David Ebert, Rachel Graham, Dean Grubbs, Michelle Heupel, Johann Mourier, Mahmood Shivji, Alison Kock, Brian Skerry, Dana Ehret, Jackie and Graham Hall, Jessica Cramp, Derek Burkholder, Jason Holmberg, Tracey Sutton, Heidi Dewar, and all the researchers, individuals, students, and research and conservation organizations featured in this book—thank you for sharing your invaluable time, expertise, experiences, photos, and passion for sharks. And to Eugenie Clark, thank you for being a beautiful light for sharks and ocean conservation, thank you for touching so many lives and making waves! —R. A. M.

Staff for This Book
Kate Olesin, Editor
Christy Ullrich Barcus, Project Editor
Julide Dengel, Art Director
Graves Fowler Creative, Designer
Jeff Heimsath, Photo Editor
Greg Ugiansky, Map Research and Production
Paige Towler, Editorial Assistant
Sanjida Rashid and Rachel Kenny, Design Production Assistants
Tammi Colleary-Loach, Rights Clearance Manager
Michael Cassady and Mari Robinson, Rights Clearance Specialists
Grace Hill, Managing Editor
Alix Inchausti, Production Editor
Lewis R. Bassford, Production Manager
Rachel Faulise, Manager, Production Services
Susan Borke, Legal and Business Affairs
Wendy Smith, Imaging

Published by the National Geographic Society
Gary E. Knell, President and CEO
John M. Fahey, Chairman of the Board
Melina Gerosa Bellows, Chief Education Officer
Declan Moore, Chief Media Officer
Hector Sierra, Senior Vice President and General Manager, Book Division

Senior Management Team, Kids Publishing and Media
Nancy Laties Feresten, Senior Vice President; Erica Green, Vice President, Editorial Director, Kids Books; Jennifer Emmett, Vice President, Content; Eva Absher-Schantz, Vice President, Visual Identity; Amanda Larsen, Design Director, Kids Books; Rachel Buchholz, Editor and Vice President, *NG Kids* magazine; Jay Sumner, Photo Director; Hannah August, Marketing Director; R. Gary Colbert, Production Director

Digital
Laura Goertzel, Manager; Sara Zeglin, Senior Producer; Bianca Bowman, Assistant Producer; Natalie Jones, Senior Product Manager

The National Geographic Society is one of the world's largest nonprofit scientific and educational organizations. Founded in 1888 to "increase and diffuse geographic knowledge," the Society's mission is to inspire people to care about the planet. It reaches more than 400 million people worldwide each month through its official journal, *National Geographic*, and other magazines; National Geographic Channel; television documentaries; music; radio; films; books; DVDs; maps; exhibitions; live events; school publishing programs; interactive media; and merchandise. National Geographic has funded more than 10,000 scientific research, conservation, and exploration projects and supports an education program promoting geographic literacy.

For more information, please visit nationalgeographic.com, call 1-800-NGS LINE (647-5463), or write to the following address:
National Geographic Society
1145 17th Street N.W.
Washington, D.C. 20036-4688 U.S.A.

Visit us online at nationalgeographic.com/books

For librarians and teachers: ngchildrensbooks.org

More for kids from National Geographic: kids.nationalgeographic.com

For information about special discounts for bulk purchases, please contact National Geographic Books Special Sales: ngspecsales@ngs.org

For rights or permissions inquiries, please contact National Geographic Books Subsidiary Rights: ngbookrights@ngs.org

Trade paperback ISBN: 978-1-4263-2090-3
Reinforced library binding: 978-1-4263-2091-0

Printed in China
15/PPS/1